The SUPERSTARS of ROCK:
Their Lives and Their Music

THE MUSIC of the great superstars has brought them fame and popularity. In this book the author brings their music to life and goes behind it to introduce the people who make the music. The Beatles, The Rolling Stones, Jimi Hendrix, Donna Summer are among the stars who come to life in these pages. Their careers are marked with excitement, suspense, and the satisfaction of success.

ALSO BY GENE BUSNAR
It's Rock 'n' Roll

The SUPER

by
GENE BUSNAR

STARS of ROCK:

Their Lives and Their Music

 JULIAN MESSNER   New York

JULIAN MESSNER and colophon are trademarks of
Simon & Schuster, registered in the U.S. Patent
and Trademark Office.

Manufactured in the United States of America.

Designed by Irving Perkins

Library of Congress Cataloging in Publication Data

Busnar, Gene.
The superstars of rock.

Bibliography: p.
Includes discographies and index.
CONTENTS: The first rock 'n' roll star: Elvis
Presley.—Super groups: TheBeattles. The Rolling
Stones. The Bee Gees.—Guitar giants: Eric Clapton.
Jimi Hendrix. [etc.]
1.   Rock musicians—Biography—Juvenile literature.
2.   Rock groups—Juvenile literature. [1.   Musicians.
2.   Rock music] I. Title.
ML3930.A2B93   784.5'4'00922 [B] [920]   80-18912
ISBN 0-671-32967-7

Acknowledgments

I would like to thank Mike Sigmund, Carl Skiba, and the rest of the staff at *Record World* for generously allowing me to use their picture files and back issues. Special thanks to Billy Vera for the rare pictures of Elvis, John Kois for his books, tapes, and Xerox machine, Barry Siegfried for his information on the Beatles, and Patti Conte of Atlantic Records for The Rolling Stones pictures. I would also like to mention my two fine editors at Messner—Iris Rosoff, who helped me get started on this project, and Jane Steltenpohl, who edited the manuscript and patiently guided the book through its many stages. I would never have completed this book without the invaluable help of my wife, Liz—thanks for everything. Finally, I would like to mention several friends who helped me through their general encouragement and/or their opinionated views on the subject of rock music—Kitty Lance, John Sposato, and Mark Schimmel.

For Elizabeth

Contents

The SUPERSTARS of ROCK:
Their Lives and Their Music

A young Elvis struts his stuff
Photo: Billy Vera collection

The First
Rock 'n' Roll
Star

1. ELVIS PRESLEY

"Paul and I wanted to be bigger than Elvis because Elvis was the thing. Whatever people say, he was it." (John Lennon in Tony Palmer's *All You Need is Love*)

ELVIS PRESLEY was much more than rock 'n' roll's first superstar. He was unquestionably the most important performer in the history of the entertainment business. His tragic death in 1977 has only served to increase his already enormous popularity. Music industry sources estimate that he will have sold 900 million records by 1980. Hundreds of imitators make a living copying Elvis's impatient singing style and hip-shaking gyrations. There are no less than three movies based on his life in production. His face still appears on the covers of national magazines, and his personal life is the focus of dozens of books. So great is Elvis's popularity that he was nominated for a Grammy Award in 1979, two years after his death.

The Presley legend, which had been fading during the last few years of his life, seems to have gained new momentum since his death. Millions of people visit Elvis's Memphis, Tennessee, grave each year to honor his memory. Hundreds of thousands more attend Elvis conventions to buy "bootleg" recordings, rare pictures, and other memorabilia. No single performer in history has been able to evoke this kind of fanatic devotion from such a wide range of fans, and it is doubtful that anyone else ever will.

There are many sides to the Elvis story — all of them fascinating. For starters, Elvis lived the American dream of going from rags to riches. He started out as a poor truck driver, but soon became the world's flashiest and most influential star.

Elvis was born in Tupelo, Mississippi, on January 8, 1935. He was the only child of Gladys and Vernon Presley, although he did have a twin brother who died at birth. Elvis began singing in church at the age of two. The family was quite poor, but Elvis's mother believed that the youngster had a talent for music and bought him a guitar for his eleventh birthday. Elvis immediately began to imitate everything he heard on the radio — country tunes, religious music, and pop ballads. When his folks weren't around, Elvis listened to the blues stylings of men like Big Bill Broonzy, Junior Parker, and Arthur "Big Boy" Cruddup. Like most God-fearing, self-respecting adults at that time, the Presleys believed this music to be vulgar and sinful. There was no way they could have known that their son's ability to sing this music would make him one of the richest and most idolized performers the world has ever known.

In 1948, when Elvis was thirteen, the Presleys moved to Memphis hoping to improve their finances. Vernon Presley, like many other poor rural farmers, felt that a move to the city would lead to a good job and a better life for his family. Instead, the Presleys wound up in a public housing project, living on welfare. When Vernon finally found a part-time job, the family almost got thrown out of the housing project. The extra income made the Presleys too rich for public assistance, though they still barely had enough money to eat. Gladys Presley had little hope for improving her lot in life, so she lived through her son. She wasn't sure just how he would do it, but she hoped and prayed that Elvis would somehow break out of the life that she and her husband were forced to endure.

There wasn't much about the teenage Elvis that revealed what he was going to become. Throughout high school, he was known as a loner who acted kind of shy. But even in those days, Elvis stood out from the crowd. His speaking manner may have been shy, but his looks were arrogant. While most of his classmates wore their hair in trim crew cuts, Elvis grew his long and combed it with globs of Vaseline into a ducktail. He also took a liking to flashy clothes and spent every spare cent he had on items like black leather jackets and red bandannas. Remember, this was a tough Tennessee high school during the early fifties. If you were going to try to stand apart from the crowd, you had better have been prepared to use your fists. Elvis's looks got him into a number of fights in those days both in and out of school. But no matter what the price, Elvis had no intention of changing his style.

During his senior year at Humes High School, Elvis entered and won the annual talent show. Nobody was aware of Elvis's musical talent before that day, but his performance made him an immediate celebrity with his peers. Suddenly, he was invited to parties every weekend and was always ready to please the crowd with a song. In the back of his mind, Elvis's dreams of becoming a performer were beginning to take shape, but they were still little more than dreams. Shortly after graduation, Elvis took a job driving a truck for the Crown Electric Company for $1.25 an hour.

Now that Elvis was bringing home fifty dollars a week,

the Presleys were able to leave the housing project for a bigger apartment in a better part of town. Elvis enjoyed life as a truck driver. His long hair and flashy clothes were not at all out of place among his co-workers. He seems to have shed much of his shyness during this period and was quite popular with the other drivers. Elvis gave most of his earnings to his parents. What little money he kept for himself was spent mostly on loud clothes and rhythm and blues records.

One of the stops on Elvis's truck route was Sun Records — a small independent label owned by a former disc jockey with an ear for black music. Sam Phillips got started in the record business by supervising recording sessions of local bluesmen like B.B. King and Howling Wolf, and leasing the finished tapes to independent companies that specialized in this kind of music. The success of a number of these records encouraged Phillips to start his own label. Within a short time, the new company had hit records with two local bluesmen — Rufus Thomas and Junior Parker. But like most rhythm and blues, these records sold almost exclusively to black listeners and were classified as "race" music.

Up until the mid-fifties, there were three well-defined and distinct categories of popular music: pop, rhythm and blues, and country. The largest in terms of both influence and wealth was pop. This music, which had remained unchanged for twenty years, consisted mostly of sentimental ballads and novelty songs. The majority of successful pop artists were crooners like Dean Martin, Perry Como, and Eddie Fisher. With their subdued beat and unemotional music, the pop records of the early fifties had about as much excitement as a bowl of overcooked mush. But the companies that released these records were owned by some of the richest corporations in America. They had done very well with the same formula for many years, and it would take a tremendous amount of pressure to force them to change. There were, however, some momentous changes taking place in America at that time which were destined to have an impact on the popular music scene.

Rhythm and blues, or "race" music, was recorded exclusively by black artists and played only on radio stations specifically geared for black audiences. For the most part, rhythm and blues was a much more lively and interesting music than pop. The lyrics were much more honest, the singing more personal and exciting, and the beat more stimulating by far. The tastes of American teenagers were beginning to differ from those of their parents. They wanted their own clothing styles, their own heroes, and their own music. As early as 1951, it was clear that a growing number of young people were becoming interested in black music. By 1952 there were a number of radio shows *on white stations* that were playing rhythm and blues. The first of these was Alan Freed's "Moondog Rock 'n' Roll House Party," which was broadcast out of Cleveland.

Country and western music was the dominant form of popular music in the South and Southwest. This was the kind of music that Elvis's parents listened to. There were a few country performers known to the national audience, primarily singing cowboys like Gene Autry and Roy Rogers. On the other hand, there were almost no artists outside the field who had C&W hits. In many ways, the country music field was even more segregated than the R&B field. This seemed to fit right in with the racial attitudes in the South at the time. Ironically, the performers who were destined to break down the barriers in popular music came from that part of America. Poor whites and blacks often worked side by side in the rural South. They shared many of the same problems and often exchanged stories and songs. This community of experiences was to become part of the basis for a new era in popular music.

Sam Phillips had a keen ear for music. But first and foremost he was a businessman. "If I could find a white singer with a black sound," he often said, "I could make a million dollars." Phillips knew that more teenagers were listening to black stations and buying rhythm and blues records every day. But Phillips rightfully understood that the commercial potential of a white rocker with an authentic sound was much greater than that of the most accomplished black blues singer. He knew that white kids wanted more than just a new sound. They wanted an artist with an image that they could relate to as their own.

One of the enterprises that Phillips ran in conjunction with Sun Records was a "cut your own disc" service. For three dollars, anyone could go into a small booth and record a song or spoken message. One Saturday afternoon in 1954, Elvis walked into the studio and asked to cut a record as a birthday present for his mother. The songs he chose were two well-known standards — "My Happiness," and "That's When My Heartaches Begin." Marion Keisker, Phillips's secretary, happened to be at the studio while Elvis was cutting his disc. Something about his style appealed to her. She felt that there might be a chance that Phillips could do something with Elvis.

When Sam Phillips heard Elvis's disc, he was not overly impressed. It is doubtful that he believed that this was the voice that would make him a million dollars. Still, he thought that there might be something there, and wanted to give the young singer a chance. In a 1957 interview in the British magazine *Hit Parader*, Elvis recalled his early days at Sun Records:

Mr. Phillips said he'd coach me if I'd come over to the studio as often as I could. It must have been a year and a half before he gave me an actual session. At last he let me try a western song — and it sounded terrible. But the second idea he had was the one that jelled.

"You want to make some blues?" he suggested over the phone, knowing I'd be a sucker for that kind of jive. He mentioned Big Boy Cruddup's name and maybe others too; I don't remember.

All I know is I hung up and ran fifteen blocks to Mr. Phillips' office before he'd gotten off the line. . . . We talked about the Cruddup records I knew — "Cool Disposition," "Rock Me Mamma," "Everything's All Right," and others. We finally settled for "That's All Right," one of my favorites . . . .

During that summer day in 1954, musical history was being made. Sam Phillips had teamed Elvis with two local musicians — guitarist Scotty Moore, and bass player Bill Black, and the three were trying to work something out in the studio. Elvis was tense. He was trying too hard. The musicians decided to take a short break and were sitting around drinking Cokes. Elvis picked up the guitar, walked over to Scotty Moore, and said, "Dig this." Half jokingly, he started to sing and play, "That's All Right." The musicians put down their drinks and began to accompany him. Suddenly, Sam Phillips ran out of the control booth screaming, "That's it, that's the sound. Now let's just try one more exactly that way." By the end of that session, Sam Phillips knew he had finally captured the sound he had been looking for. The problem was finding somebody with enough guts to play it on the radio.

The local Memphis disc jockeys agreed with Phillips. This was a good record, and that Presley kid sure did put the tune over. But the song couldn't be played on the country-and-western stations; the sound was too black. On the other hand, Elvis was white, so the black disc jockeys weren't really interested either. But Phillips was persistent.

He finally convinced a local disc jockey named Dewey Phillips (no relation) to play the record. The response was tremendous. People wrote letters and called in requesting the song. Some of the listeners had heard rumors that the singer was actually a white boy and started referring to Elvis as, "the hillbilly cat."

It is doubtful that many contemporary listeners would actually mistake Elvis for a black man, though it is clear that he was strongly influenced by the great blues singers. In fact, Elvis had a completely unique way of singing the blues. His style was not based on crying and sulking about his sorrows. Rather, he seemed to be using the music to declare his personal freedom and independence. While most of the traditional bluesmen moaned about their troubles, Elvis celebrated his liberation. Nobody had ever heard a white man sing that way on the radio. Many people were outraged that white stations were playing this music, but it was too late to stem the tide. The music of the South, like its schools and buses, was becoming integrated.

Elvis recorded a total of ten songs for the Sun Label between 1954–55. Each two-sided single contained a blues song backed with a traditional country tune. Sam Phillips wanted to cover his investment. If the blues sides proved too offensive, he would simply ask the disc jockeys to turn the record over. Elvis was a good country singer, but his sound was not especially unique on this kind of material. He was at his best on the blues cuts where his excited and impatient singing style was most effective.

With each succeeding release on the Sun Label, Elvis's popularity grew. Each record sold more than the previous one, and some of the country sides became hits on their own. Elvis was also "knocking them dead" at live performances throughout the South, though he was still unknown in other parts of the country. By the summer of 1955, Elvis had caught the eyes and the ears of the Northern music establishment. Thanks to the carefully planned wheeling and dealing of his new manager, Colonel Tom Parker, several of the major record companies entered into a bidding war attempting to buy out Elvis's recording contract with Sun. The eventual winner was RCA Records, who shelled out forty thousand dollars to Sam Phillips for Elvis's recording rights. This was a huge sum of money for that time.

Although Elvis was now on the threshold of international fame and fortune, many rock 'n' roll purists believed that he had reached his musical peak on the Sun recordings. These critics did not object to Elvis's moving to a bigger label. Even Sam Phillips understood that Elvis's potential was too big to be properly exploited by a small regional company. It was, rather, the change in his singing that upset these listeners.

Charlie Gillet—author of the excellent book, *The Sound of the City*—is among those who prefer the Sun cuts to any of the recordings on RCA:

> [On his blues sides with the Sun label] Elvis evolved a personal version of the blues style, singing high and clear, breathless, and impatient, varying his rhythmic emphasis with a confidence and inventiveness that were exceptional for a white singer. The sound suggested a young white man celebrating his freedom, ready to do anything, go anywhere, pausing long enough for apologies and even regrets, but then hustling on toward the new. At RCA under the supervision of Chet Atkins, Presley's records featured vocal groups, heavily electrified guitars, and drums (instead of the simple accompaniment of Scotty Moore's guitar and Bill Black's bass). Responding to these unfamiliar intrusions in his accompaniment, Presley's voice became more theatrical and self-conscious as he sought to contrive excitement and emotion which he seemed to achieve on his Sun records without any evident forethought.

This writer agrees with Gillet's analysis up to a point. It is certainly true that the Sun cuts have a simple purity in both the vocals and instrumental backing which is lacking in Elvis's later work. Still, it would be hard to choose between the Sun cuts and some of Elvis's early records for RCA. Songs like "Heartbreak Hotel," "Hound Dog," and "Don't Be Cruel" hold up as well as any early rock 'n' roll. The Sun cuts are true rockabilly — a cross between blues and hillbilly. But the early RCA records can only be called rock 'n' roll. It is true that the heavy drum beat and the amplified guitars caused Elvis to sing in a louder and gruffer voice, but who is to say that this was any less original than the voice he used on the Sun cuts.

The final decision as to which Elvis records show him at his true peak comes down to a question of personal taste. One thing is for certain — Elvis's singing with RCA provided him with the opportunity to become the first nationally acclaimed rock 'n' roll star. Many of his records topped the pop, R&B, and country charts. During 1956, Elvis had five of the year's top-twenty records. His first release on the new label, "Heartbreak Hotel," sold well over a million copies. A few months later, Elvis became the first artist in the history of the music business to have both the number one and the number two records at the same time. As if this weren't enough, the two songs — "Hound Dog," and "Don't Be Cruel," were the A and B sides of the same record.

Elvis was clearly the biggest thing to ever hit the music business. So phenomenal were his record sales that RCA had to rent its competitors' record pressing facilities to keep up with the demand. Record companies searched frantically for singers who sounded like Elvis, and often settled for someone who just looked like him. Not surprisingly, Sam Phillips was the most successful in signing and recording other good rockabilly performers. As soon as Elvis left the label, Phillips signed Carl Perkins — who wrote and recorded the original version of "Blue Suede Shoes." He also had Jerry Lee Lewis — the frantic singing piano player who had a number of huge hits, including "Whole Lot of Shakin' Goin' On," and "Great Balls of Fire." But as great as these men were, Elvis was still the undisputed king of rock 'n' roll.

Throughout 1956, Elvis was the rebellious idol of millions of American teenagers. His concerts produced a hysteria which far surpassed that caused by Frank Sinatra during the forties. It wasn't only his music, but his sneering mouth and wiggling hips that appealed to his young fans. During those years, Elvis belonged exclusively to the teenagers — boys as well as girls, Northerners as well as Southerners, blacks as well as whites.

Elvis' popularity was bolstered by a number of TV appearances, first on the Tommy Dorsey and Jackie Gleason

Elvis with a few of his adoring fans
Photo: Billy Vera collection

shows, and then on the Milton Berle and Steve Allen shows. The producers of some of these programs were extremely uptight about Elvis's body movements and insisted that he be shown only from the waist up. Ed Sullivan, who hosted TV's highest rated variety show vowed that he would never allow a performer as vulgar as Elvis to appear on his stage. But even he relented and signed Elvis for three appearances at seventeen thousand dollars per show.

While teenagers viewed the Presley explosion as the most exciting event of their lives, many adults were appalled. The music he was singing was okay for dimly lit rhythm and blues clubs. But here was this defiant and sexual white youth singing this music and moving his body suggestively on Ed Sullivan's TV show. Something would have to be done before all of America's youth became corrupted.

The older generation spoke of rock 'n' roll in terms of "jungle music" and "voodoo." They feared that the heavy beat and the loud volume of "that pagan music" would turn their children into juvenile delinquents and worse. Adults often cited a 1954 report that spoke of the rising state of teenage crime. Two films, *The Wild One*, with Marlon Brando, and *Rebel without a Cause*, with James Dean, addressed themselves to this topic. Although the heroes of both films had haircuts and sideburns which closely resembled Elvis's, the background music for these movies was jazz, not rock 'n' roll. But when the 1955 movie *Blackboard Jungle* appeared with Bill Haley's "Rock Around the Clock" as its theme song, the link between juvenile delinquency and rock 'n' roll became established.

Although there is little or no evidence that rock 'n' roll caused young people to become violent, the music did inspire aggressive behavior on the part of some adults. Their protests against rock 'n' roll led to bans, arrests, and physical destruction. "Smash those records which present a pagan way of life," urged one magazine. "Some singers need a good swift kick. So do the songwriters. So do the disc jockeys," it went on to say.

Not all of this hostility was directed toward Elvis, but his mushrooming popularity presented the greatest threat to those who wished to destroy rock 'n' roll. One Chicago disc jockey smashed Elvis's records over the air. Another platter spinner in Buffalo, New York, was fired for playing Presley records. A number of used car dealers guaranteed to break one hundred Elvis records with every car purchased. Elvis was nicknamed "the Pelvis," and there seemed to be a concerted effort by certain people to "get him."

But Elvis and his manager Colonel Tom Parker were three steps ahead of their enemies. In sharp contrast to his defiant sneer and sexy gyrations, Elvis was a polite country boy who always addressed his elders as sir and ma'am. He also knew how to sing the kind of songs that would appeal to the members of the older generation. By the end of 1956, Elvis recorded his first ballad, "Love Me Tender." The song which was in a soft and easy style sold over 850,000 copies before it was ever released. *Love Me Tender* was also the title of the first of thirty Presley movies.

The ever astute Colonel Parker signed his boy to three movies for Paramount Pictures. These early films set the pattern which was to be followed for years: Find a stock plot; make the acting simple; and leave some predictable spaces for Elvis to sing. These movies were often made on a low budget. Thus, the percentage that Elvis and the Colonel wound up with came to millions of dollars. Also, there was always an album of songs released from each movie. This meant more money from both record sales and song publishing fees.

In later years, Elvis wanted to try more serious acting. It is even possible that he had the talent to become a competent actor. But the Colonel would not hear of it. Every one of Elvis's formula movies had been a financial success. No great actor could make that claim — not Marlon Brando, John Wayne, or Gary Cooper. Colonel Parker felt that his role was to make Elvis (and himself) as much money as possible, and nothing was going to stand in his way. The Colonel always liked to say: "When I met that boy, he had a million dollars worth of talent. Now he has a million dollars."

By the end of 1956, the Colonel had made every possible kind of marketing deal for Elvis Presley products. There were Elvis Presley clothes, Elvis Presley handkerchiefs, Elvis Presley necklaces, guitars, dolls, buttons, combs, pillows, and bookends. There were many other items, including stuffed hound dogs, and heartbreak hotels. On every one of these gimmicks, Elvis and the Colonel received a royalty of somewhere between five-to-ten percent. This amounted to millions of dollars before the end of the fifties. Since Elvis's death, the value of these items has skyrocketed beyond anything even the Colonel could have imagined.

The relationship between Elvis and his manager had a great bearing on the star's career. In purely financial terms, Tom Parker must be considered a genius. But it is questionable whether the moves he made truly benefited Elvis as an artist and as a person. By the end of 1956, Elvis could have released any kind of record and sold a million copies. Why then didn't he continue to develop his unique style by making good, solid rock 'n' roll records? Like a number of other great artists, Elvis did not really understand where his greatest talent lay. Unwilling or unable to make his own career decisions, he chose to let the Colonel make them instead. But Elvis was just a young country boy who got caught up in events that would have confused a much older and wiser person.

Colonel Parker, however, wasn't confused in the least. He knew how to reap the most out of every turn in Elvis's career. When Elvis was drafted into the army in 1958, the Colonel wisely used the publicity to build up his star's image as the all-American boy. When the army offered Elvis a chance to perform in its special services division, the Colonel said, "no thanks." Elvis patriotically insisted that he be treated just like any other new recruit, but the crafty Colonel had his own reasons for not wanting Elvis to perform. Special services performers did not receive pay, and this went against the Colonel's grain. "If they want my boy to sing," he is reported to have said, "they're going to have to pay just like anyone else."

For most performers, two years away from their public would be a disaster. But Elvis Presley wasn't most performers. Every move he made in the army was a news headline. Elvis's public image was changing from teenage hood to patriotic soldier. The Colonel knew that the groundwork was being laid for a new Presley image. Soon his audiences would include the middle-aged and old, as well as the young.

Six months after Elvis's induction into the army, Gladys Presley died of a heart attack due to hepatitis. Elvis had been extremely close to his mother, and her death left him shattered. Much has been made of the effect this tragedy had on Elvis's personality. Many of his friends believe that the problems he had during the last few years of his life would have not been as severe had his mother lived. Ironically, Elvis's premature death occurred at exactly the same age as his mother's, forty-two.

Upon his release from the army in 1960, Elvis resumed his movie making career. For the next eight years, he did not perform live. His work in Hollywood occupied most of his time. Most of the records released during that period were the rather corny soundtracks from movies like *Blue Hawaii, Roustabout, Fun in Acapulco, Wild in the Country,* and *Follow That Dream.* Had any of these films featured an actor other than Elvis in the lead, it is doubtful that people would have paid ten cents to see them. But since it *was* Elvis who was singing and running around some tropical beach with a gorgeous leading lady, the fans lined up, paid their money, and bought the soundtrack album.

Elvis may have been getting rich from his movies, but he was also getting bored. The work was not at all challenging, and Elvis needed a challenge. He also needed the reassurance that he could turn on a live audience. During the years he had been away, the Beatles had taken his place as the top rock 'n' roll act in the world. In fact, Elvis had become somewhat of a joke to serious rock 'n' roll listeners. While the audience had nurtured and developed its taste for good rock 'n' roll, Elvis had degenerated into somewhat of a singing clown with records like "Bossa Nova Baby," and "Rock-A-Hula Baby."

But in 1968 Elvis staged a comeback which was both daring and remarkable. It had been decided that Elvis would do a Christmas special on TV to be broadcast internationally. The Colonel wanted the show to be a formal affair, with Elvis in a tuxedo singing Christmas songs. But Elvis insisted on a tough and gritty show. Together with Steve Binder, the producer of the program, Elvis finally convinced the Colonel to let him do it his way.

When Elvis appeared on the stage that night, it was as if that tough rock 'n' roller from Memphis had never left. Dressed in a black leather jacket, and surrounded by a responsive, if somewhat hand-picked, audience, Elvis proved that he had lost none of his greatness. Together with the members of his original combo, Elvis made some of the best music of his career that night. In between his songs, Elvis joked about the Beatles and denied that they had surpassed him. He also recalled, with some bitterness, a time in Florida when the police forced him to sing without moving. But for this one night, Elvis was going to do it *his* way. In his remarkable book, *Mystery Train*, writer Greil Marcus recalls the magic of Elvis's performance that night:

> Shouting, crying, growling, lusting, Elvis takes his stand and the crowd takes theirs with him, no longer reaching for the past they had been brought to the studio to reenact, but responding to something completely new. The crowd is cheering for what they had only hoped for: Elvis has gone beyond all their expectations and his, and they don't believe it. The guitar cuts in high and slams down and Elvis is roaring. Every line is a thunderbolt. AW, YEAH! screams a pal — he has waited years for this moment. . . . It was the finest music of his life. If there was ever music that bleeds, this was it. Nothing came easy that night, and he gave everything he had — more than anyone knew was there.

After the television special, Elvis made a comeback album, *From Elvis in Memphis*, which was his best in years. A single off the album, "Suspicious Minds," became his first number-one hit in a long time. He now felt ready to return to live performing. He hungered for the love and adulation of a real audience. The location for Elvis's return to the live stage was the International Hotel in Las Vegas.

Again Elvis proved up to the challenge of meeting his public head-on. The show had sold out immediately. Fans came from as far away as Australia to see the King perform. The show was a financial success before Elvis ever walked out on the stage, but there were some doubts about his comeback. Would he be able to handle a live audience? Was Las Vegas the right place to bring him back? It was immediately clear that the answer to these questions was a resounding yes.

When Elvis leaped on the stage singing "Blue Suede Shoes," the twenty-five-hundred fans began screaming and applauding. They were dancing in the aisles as Elvis wailed through "Heartbreak Hotel," "Jailhouse Rock," "Love Me Tender," and the rest of his best-known songs. The excitement that Elvis generated that night was magnified since Las Vegas audiences were usually somewhat reserved. But this was something special: *The King was back.*

An ecstatic Colonel Parker worked out a five-year deal with the International Hotel for an astronomical sum. Elvis was to perform at the hotel several times a year. In addition, the Colonel arranged bookings in major halls throughout the country.

The new Elvis Presley was not merely a rock 'n' roll singer. His sets included every type of song that was part of American life — country ballads, pop tunes, religious gospel music, patriotic songs, and rock 'n' roll. It was as if Elvis were holding up the American dream with all its myths for the world to see. Dressed in a red, white, and blue outfit, draped with a Superman cape, and covered with jewels, Elvis seemed to be laughing at the myth he had become. He had taken all that America had to offer and now was displaying it to his audiences' apparent delight.

But Elvis quickly became bored with live performing. He grew lazy and refused to learn new songs. At times, he would even announce to the audience that he hadn't learned the words to a song and would read them off an index card. It is not difficult to understand Elvis's boredom. He had, after all, reached his artistic peak almost twenty years earlier, and it was unlikely that he would break any new musical ground. By the early seventies, he spent much of his time on stage merely going through the motions.

Things were also not going well in Elvis's personal life. After his wife, Priscilla, left him in 1972, Elvis's problems began making the front pages of the gossip magazines. He had put on a great deal of weight. There was also talk that he consumed large quantities of pills — amphetamines to elevate his mood and kill his appetite, and barbiturates to calm him down and put him to sleep. There was a good deal of irony to these rumors, since President Nixon had made Elvis an honorary official of the Federal Drug Enforcement Bureau in 1971.

The King—Paunchy and close to the end
Record World—RCA Records

From his earliest days as a star, Elvis surrounded himself with a number of friends from Memphis. This group, which was known as the Memphis Mafia, was with Elvis constantly. Members served as bodyguards, companions, and stunt men in his movies. When three of these men — Red West, Dave Hebler, and Sonny West — were fired in 1976, they collaborated with writer Steve Dunleavy on a book entitled *Elvis, What Happened?* Many of the revelations in this book ring true. But it would also be wise to keep in mind that these men did not make a great deal of money when they worked for Elvis, and they may have been bitter when they were fired.

According to his three former bodyguards, Elvis started out as a simple downhome country boy and ended up a man who was totally corrupted and destroyed by his fame. The book, which came out only weeks before Elvis's death, confirmed the rumors that Elvis indeed had a serious drug problem which had nearly killed him several times in the recent past. It also painted the picture of a violent, brooding man who would shoot a bullet through a television set if he didn't like the program. There are countless stories of Elvis's cruelty toward the people around him, his obsession with his own power, and his degenerate lifestyle.

There are also numerous stories of Elvis's great generosity. It is well known that he would buy Cadillacs for all his friends when he went on a buying spree. At times, he would even buy new cars and jewelry for fans that he had never met before. He was, his former friends claim, a man who needed love so badly that he would sometimes hand out diamond rings to an audience in order to get them to respond.

Whatever Elvis was or became, he was in great part a product of his circumstances. Can a poor country boy suddenly become the world's biggest star and still keep his feet on the ground? It is not easy to become the idol of millions. Such a person can never simply take a walk or go to a movie. Elvis was so well known that he couldn't even go out during the daylight hours without being mobbed by fans. It also became difficult for him to tell who his real friends were and who was hanging around just for the money. Even so, this does not excuse some of the things that Elvis's former bodyguards claim he did. It merely explains how too much power and fame can lead to problems.

Whenever a man dies at the age of forty-two, it is always a tragic event. Sadly, it is not an unusually young age for a rock 'n' roll death. There are far too many examples of rock performers who died in their twenties — Jimi Hendrix, Janis Joplin, Brian Jones, Duane Allman, Otis Redding, and Jim Morrison — to name a few. Whether these performers died from drugs, like Janis or Jimi, or in a plane crash like Otis, their death was in no small measure fueled by their success. Perhaps these tragedies will serve as a warning to others who seek the limelight. There are so many problems connected with stardom, particularly if the star in question isn't strong enough or mature enough to handle its pitfalls.

A sad footnote to the Elvis Presley story is that he apparently died alone. Of course, his fans still love him, maybe more than ever. But it seems there was no one really close to him at the time of his death. Still, Elvis will not be forgotten by the millions of people whose lives he touched and changed. It will probably be years until his true importance is recognized. Greil Marcus has called him "the supreme figure in American life, one whose presence brooks no real comparison."

As far as Elvis's contributions to popular music are concerned, there is little doubt that he remains the pivotal figure in rock history. Chet Atkins, who produced Elvis's early sessions at RCA, summed up his importance this way:

He brought in a new era and there were so many spin-offs from his music. Before Elvis it was gospel, country, pop, and rhythm and blues. All of a sudden here comes a white guy who does black music, and he becomes socially acceptable to white kids where maybe a black artist wouldn't be at that time. I don't think a thing like that will ever happen again. There were these four or five separate musics, and all of a sudden they started to fuse together. They're still moving together, still merging, until now who can tell the difference between a Waylon Jennings record and a James Taylor record. They are not that much different. I think a lot of young people don't realize that Elvis had that impact, and I think they should.

I don't think there will ever be another like him, not in my time certainly. The rock 'n' roll era has lasted 22 years, much longer than any music that I know of and I think Elvis was responsible for that, like it or not.

ELVIS PRESLEY COLLECTORS' GUIDE

— Smash Hit

SELECTED ALBUMS

Year	Album	Label	Hit
1958	*Elvis's Golden Records*	RCA Victor	*
1960	*Elvis's Golden Records Volume 2*	RCA Victor	*
1963	*Elvis's Golden Records Volume 3*	RCA Victor	*
1968	*Elvis's Golden Records Volume 4*	RCA Victor	*
1970	*Elvis's Worldwide 50 Gold Award Hits Volume I*	RCA Victor	*
1971	*Worldwide Gold Award Hits Volume II*	RCA Victor	*

SINGLES

Year	Single	Label	Hit
1954	That's All Right/Blue Moon of Kentucky	Sun	
1954	Good Rockin' Tonight/I Don't Care if the Sun Don't Shine	Sun	
1955	Milkcow Blues Boogie/You're a Heartbreaker	Sun	
1955	Baby Let's Play House/I'm Left, Your Right, She's Gone	Sun	
1955	Mystery Train/I Forgot to Remember to Forget	Sun	
1956	Heartbreak Hotel/I Was the One	RCA Victor	*
1956	Blue Suede Shoes	RCA Victor	*
1956	I Want You, I Need You, I Love You/My Baby Left Me	RCA Victor	*
1956	Don't Be Cruel	RCA Victor	*
1956	Hound Dog	RCA Victor	*
1956	Love Me Tender/Anyway You Want Me (That's How I Will Be)	RCA Victor	*
1956	Love Me/When My Blue Moon Turns to Gold Again	RCA Victor	*
1956	Poor Boy	RCA Victor	
1956	Old Shep	RCA Victor	
1957	Too Much/Playing for Keeps	RCA Victor	*
1957	All Shook Up/That's When Your Heartaches Begin	RCA Victor	*
1957	(There'll Be) Peace in the Valley	RCA Victor	
1957	Let Me Be Your Teddy Bear/Loving You	RCA Victor	*
1957	Jailhouse Rock	RCA Victor	*
1957	Treat Me Nice	RCA Victor	*
1958	Don't/I Beg of You	RCA Victor	*
1958	Wear My Ring Around Your Neck/Doncha' Think Its Time	RCA Victor	*

SINGLES

Year	Single	Label	Hit
1958	Hard Headed Woman/Don't Ask Me Why	RCA Victor	*
1958	One Night/I Got Stung	RCA Victor	*
1958	(Now and Then There's) A Fool Such as I/I Need Your Love Tonight	RCA Victor	*
1959	A Big Hunk O'Love/My Wish Came True	RCA Victor	*
1960	Stuck on You/Fame and Fortune	RCA Victor	*
1960	It's Now or Never/A Mess Blues	RCA Victor	*
1960	Are You Lonesome Tonight/I Gotta Know	RCA Victor	*
1961	Surrender	RCA Victor	*
1961	Flaming Star	RCA Victor	*
1961	I Feel So Bad/Wild in the Streets	RCA Victor	*
1961	(Marie's the Name) His Latest Flame/Little Sister	RCA Victor	*
1961	Can't Help Falling in Love/Rock-A-Hula Baby	RCA Victor	*
1962	Good Luck Charm/Anything That's Part of You	RCA Victor	*
1962	Follow That Dream	RCA Victor	*
1962	She's Not You	RCA Victor	*
1962	King of the Whole Wide World	RCA Victor	
1962	Return to Sender	RCA Victor	*
1963	One Broken Heart for Sale	RCA Victor	*
1963	(You're the) Devil in Disguise	RCA Victor	*
1963	Bossa Nova Baby/Witchcraft	RCA Victor	*
1964	Kissin' Cousins/It Hurts Me	RCA Victor	*
1964	Such a Night	RCA Victor	*
1964	Ask Me/Ain't That Loving You	RCA Victor	*
1965	Crying in the Chapel	RCA Victor	*
1965	(Such An) Easy Question	RCA Victor	*
1965	I'm Yours	RCA Victor	*
1965	Puppet on a String	RCA Victor	*

SINGLES

Year	Single	Label	Hit
1966	*Love Letters*	RCA Victor	*
1968	*If I Can Dream*	RCA Victor	*
1969	*In the Ghetto*	RCA Victor	*
1969	*Suspicious Minds*	RCA Victor	*
1969	*Don't Cry Daddy*	RCA Victor	*
1970	*The Wonder of You*	RCA Victor	*
1970	*Kentucky Rain*	RCA Victor	*
1970	*You Don't Have to Say You Love Me*	RCA Victor	*
1970	*I Really Don't Want to Know*	RCA Victor	*
1972	*Burning Love*	RCA Victor	*
1972	*Separate Ways*	RCA Victor	*
1973	*Steamroller Blues/Fool*	RCA Victor	*
1974	*If You Talk in Your Sleep*	RCA Victor	*
1975	*Trouble*	RCA Victor	
1975	*Pieces of My Life*	RCA Victor	
1975	*My Boy*	RCA Victor	*
1975	*Bringing It Back*	RCA Victor	

Supergroups

2. THE BEATLES

THE BEATLES are gone but not forgotten. More than a decade after their breakup, they are still as popular as ever. Just turn on the radio: Top-40 stations and progressive FM stations still play their records constantly; jazz musicians make instrumental versions of their songs, and easy-listening performers turn Beatle music into Beatle muzak. Nobody in the history of popular music ever caused this much of an impact. Neither John Lennon, Paul McCartney, George Harrison, nor Ringo Starr had all the ingredients to become a superstar on his own. But together, they achieved things that no single artist ever could.

The reasons for the Beatle explosion in the sixties are simple enough to understand. The group came along at just the right time with a fresh musical sound and a refreshing outlook on life. Many rock historians have remarked that rock was in danger of dying before the Beatles hit the scene.

"They changed rock, which changed the culture, which changed us." (*New York Times*)
Record World—Capitol Records

But in fact, there were many good records on the radio at that time. Most of the really good singers were black, and this tended to limit their appeal in those days. Also, many of the performers were controlled by their producers. As great as the records of the Crystals, and the Ronettes were, Phil Spector wrote, arranged, produced, and received most of the recognition for this music. But the Beatles were unique. They absorbed all this good stuff that was going on in America and added their own distinctive touch. A number of their early records were covers of recent hits like Smokey Robinson's "You've Really Got a Hold on Me," Barrett Strong's "Money," and the Marvelettes's "Please Mr. Postman." But the Beatles wrote many of their early hits. Also, they played, arranged, and sang on all of their records. As the first self-contained group to become popular, they opened the door for The Rolling Stones, The Who, and a thousand lesser bands.

It was clear from the start that the Beatles learned their

craft from the great rock 'n' roll artists of the fifties. They started out by copying the styles of Elvis, Chuck Berry, Little Richard, Buddy Holly, and the Everly Brothers; but they took this music a step further. Lennon and McCartney had a unique way of writing and a completely fresh vocal sound. Even on their earliest tunes, they displayed a tongue-in-cheek humor and their own kind of intelligence. There was a lot more going on below the surface than song titles like "I Want to Hold Your Hand" and "She Loves You" would suggest. Also, it was somewhat of a novelty to hear Englishmen singing rock 'n' roll.

Before the Beatles, rock 'n' roll was strictly an American phenomenon. There were a number of Elvis imitators in England during the late fifties and early sixties, but their records were rarely heard outside of Britain. On the other hand, many famous American rock-'n'-rollers were even more popular with the English youth than with audiences in their own country. But the Beatles changed all this. After they took the world by storm, England became *the* vital center for rock 'n' roll.

By the end of the sixties, the Beatles had converted the whole world to rock 'n' roll. Thousands of older listeners who had disregarded R&B and laughed at Elvis's gyrations became Beatle fanatics. Part of the reason for this mass appeal was that much of their music was really closer to traditional pop than to rock 'n' roll. Songs like "Yesterday," "Michelle," and "Something" were smooth ballads with no trace of a rock beat. Just as many older listeners were ready to accept the Beatles' rock songs as "good music," the died-in-the-wool rock fans had no problem digging these soft ballads. As long as it was the Beatles, everyone wanted as much as they could get.

No performers could achieve such widespread acceptance on musical grounds alone. In fact, the first couple of Beatle records released in America did not go anywhere. People needed to see them and hear them speak in order to understand what was really going on. In 1963, the atmosphere in America was grim. When President John F. Kennedy was assassinated, a great deal of the hope and optimism of the young died as well. Something new was needed to revive us, and the Beatles were that something.

Everything about them was right. Their long hair, their wry humor, and their English accents. A great part of their collective charm came from their refusal to take themselves or anything else seriously. They enjoyed making fun of all conventions and particularly relished giving certain members of the press a hard time. Here are some excerpts from a typical Beatle press conference in the early sixties:

> Reporter: "Where did you get the name the Beatles?"
> John: "I thought of it."
> Reporter: "Do you fight among yourselves?"
> Ringo: "Only in the morning."
> Reporter: "What do you think of criticism that you're not
>   very good?"
> Paul: "They're right; we're not."
> Reporter: "What do you call that haircut?"
> George: "I call it Arthur."

As John, Paul, George, and Ringo created the kind of chaos formerly seen only in Marx Brothers movies, young people adopted them as their unofficial leaders. Rock 'n' roll was no longer just some catchy music coming out of the radio. It was the most important thing about being young. Elvis had deserted rock 'n' roll after a few short years. But the Beatles were genuinely connected to their audience. They shared the same attitudes, the same hopes, and many of the same problems. By 1965 their albums became regarded as major cultural events. A generation looked to the Beatles in order to see themselves.

THE EARLY YEARS

ALL FOUR Beatles grew up in working-class families in the city of Liverpool. From the start, John Lennon was the musical and intellectual leader of the group. Although he was an intelligent and creative child who wrote and sketched satirical pamphlets, John was pretty much a cutup at school. By the time he enrolled in Quarry Bank High School, he had organized his own gang. John and his friends spent most of their time pulling pranks, harassing teachers, and getting into fights. But when his mother bought him a guitar and showed him a few chords, John discovered a new outlet for his creativity and his aggressions.

During the fifties, a musical style called "skiffle" became popular in England. This music was a loose combination of folk and jug band styles. Most of the instruments used in a skiffle band were makeshift items like washboards and tea chests. The only conventional instrument was a guitar, and a few simple chords were usually enough to get by. Like hundreds of other teenagers throughout England, John organized his own skiffle group. They were called the Quarrymen.

John didn't know yet where his music would lead him, but he was sure of the image he wanted. He had seen American movies about rebellious youth like *Rebel without a Cause,* and *Blackboard Jungle,* and copied the tough-guy styles of these films. The Quarrymen all wore leather jackets, tight pants, and greasy ducktail haircuts. James Dean was one of their heroes. But most of all, Lennon admired Elvis. "Nothing really affected me until Elvis," he told Beatles' biographer Hunter Davies. Almost immediately, the group began playing at local dances, dreaming of the day they would become rock 'n' roll stars. Then, on June 15, 1956, one of the Quarrymen brought along a friend to hear the band. His name was James Paul McCartney.

John was very impressed with Paul right from the start. For one thing, he had the right look. Paul wore a skin-tight pair of black pants and a white jacket. With his baby face and jet black hair, Paul looked more than a little bit like Elvis. He was also ahead of John musically and was able to show off by playing a few popular rock 'n' roll songs on the guitar. John sensed that Paul had the kind of strong personality that would complement his own. A short time later he invited Paul to join the Quarrymen. As they got closer, Paul showed John some original songs he had written. Soon the two were writing together.

While Paul was attending high school at the Liverpool Institute, he became friendly with George Harrison. Although he was several years younger than John or Paul, George was a much more accomplished guitar player than either of them. "It was too much," John told Hunter Davies. "George was just too young. I didn't want to know him at first. . . . George looked even younger than Paul, and Paul looked about ten with his baby face." But when John heard how well George could play, he eventually changed his mind and asked him to join the Quarrymen.

For the next year or two they would all get together at Paul's house and jam. John and Paul had written over a hundred songs including "Love Me Do," which was to become their first hit single. During that time, John suffered a severe emotional blow when his mother was run over by a car. Friends report that he became bitter, and even violent. But the tragedy also helped to cement his relationship with Paul, who had also recently lost his mother.

In spite of all the trouble that marked John's days at Quarry Bank High School, he somehow managed to get enrolled at the Liverpool College of Art. There, he formed a close friendship with Stu Sutcliffe, a talented art student. When Stu won some prize money in an art exhibition, John suggested how he might put it to good use. Stu was always hanging around when John and the others would practice. This was his chance to become one of them. John, Paul, and George all fancied themselves as front men, but they needed some backing. Stu was encouraged to buy a bass guitar. It didn't matter that he had no idea how to play the instrument; they would teach him.

The band went through a series of names, including Wump and the Werbles, the Rainbows, and Johnny and the Moondogs. They had totally lost their interest in skiffle, and had acquired electric guitars and amplifiers. Now that they were a rock 'n' roll band, John decided that it was time for a new name. He had always been a great admirer of Buddy Holly's group, the Crickets. So, he tried to think up a similar name. The music that the local rock groups played was often called "beat" music; that's how John devised the name — BEATles.

The band's first real job was a two-week tour of Scotland backing a singer named Johnny Gentle. When they returned to Liverpool, they worked at a number of local clubs. One of these clubs was called the Casbah, owned by a Mrs. Best. Her son, Pete, was an aspiring drummer whose band had recently broken up. When the Beatles were offered an extended engagement in Hamburg, Germany, they enlisted the services of Pete Best. At last, they had all the ingredients of a real rock 'n' roll band.

The decision to go to Hamburg was an important turning point in the Beatles' young lives. They were prepared to leave their families, friends, and schools behind in order to pursue their dreams. This experience would change their lives and their music dramatically.

The first club they worked in Hamburg was called the Indra. They were required to play six nights a week, eight hours a night. In order to keep the dancers happy, they often had to stretch a song out for an hour. This grueling routine wore them out physically, and they often had to take pep pills to stay up. But the Beatles developed more musically in those five months than they ever could have imagined. Because this was a do-or-die situation in which they were forced to pound out song after marathon song, the Beatles were able to experiment, and eventually refine their sound.

The young men learned about many things in Hamburg besides music. During the early sixties, that city was known as the vice capital of Europe. The streets were full of strip joints and prostitutes, and the clubs were the centers of wild drunken fights. This was quite an education for a group of teenagers so far away from home. Much of the craziness carried over to the Beatles stage performance. John would often wear long underwear and a toilet seat around his neck, while shouting obscenities at the audience. He remembers the scene at the Indra this way:

> We hated the club owners so much that we jumped around until we broke through the stage. We'd all end up jumpin' round on the floor. Paul would be singing "What'd I Say" for an hour and a half. All these gangsters would come in like the Mafia. They'd just send a crate of this sort of cheap German champagne onstage, and we'd have to drink it, though it killed us. They'd say, "Drink it and then do 'What'd I Say'".... If they came in at five in the morning and we'd been playing for seven hours, they gave us a crate of champagne, and we were supposed to carry on. I used to get so (drunk), I'd be lyin' on the floor in back of the piano while the rest of the group was playing.

During those months in Hamburg the Beatles became close with two young German artists — Klaus Voornam and Astrid Kichener. Within a short time, Stu and Astrid became romantically involved and got engaged. Astrid was fascinated by the Beatles and took several hundred pictures of them. She soon convinced Stu to let her cut his Elvis-inspired hair. Astrid shaped it into a shorter neater look with slight bangs over the front. John, Paul, and George soon followed suit. This hair style later became known as the Beatle cut.

The group was doing so well at the Indra that they were offered a job at a better club for more money. Suddenly, the roof caved in. George was discovered to be under age and was promptly deported. Paul and Pete Best accidentally started a fire, and they too were thrown out of Germany. John had to sell his clothes and borrow money from Astrid in order to get back to Liverpool. The Beatles were so depressed and dejected that they actually considered packing it in.

After a few weeks of sulking, the group got back together and decided to get the show on the road again. They found that they were extremely popular in Liverpool. Their Hamburg experiences had turned them into a tight, tough rock band. Their audiences became so enthused that there were often riots when they played. Already, local papers were calling them "a phenomenon which would not happen again."

The Liverpool club at which the Beatles appeared the most was the Cavern. They played there throughout 1961, except for a brief engagement at the Top Ten Club in Hamburg. While they were in Germany, they made their first records backing up singer Tony Sheridan. Shortly before the recording session, Stu left the group in order to continue with his art studies. Although he was an important intellectual influence on the other Beatles, Stu wasn't really up to par as a musician. He was rather embarrassed about his limited skills as a bass player and often stood with his back to the audience in order to hide his deficiencies. He was a very talented artist though, and his decision to return to art school would have probably been for the best. Tragically, Stu developed a brain hemorrhage and died several months later. John was particularly saddened by his death. "I depended on him to tell me the truth," he told Hunter Davies. "Stu would tell me if something was good and I would believe him."

The Beatles were back in the Cavern again, with Paul now handling the bass guitar chores. They were pretty well settled into their routine, but things were about to turn around once again. In November 1961, several fans came into Nems Music Store and asked for a record called "My Bonnie" by Tony Sheridan and the Beatles. The man behind the counter was Brian Epstein, head of the record department in one of his family's stores. Epstein had never heard of the Beatles, but he made it a matter of policy to fill all customer requests. The number of requests for "My Bonnie" was growing, and so was Epstein's curiosity. When he learned that the Beatles were a local group, he decided to go to the Cavern and see them. Although he found the club "dark, damp, and smelly, and the noise deafening," Epstein decided he was interested in getting to know the group.

After several lunchtime visits to the Cavern, Epstein offered the group a management contract. The Beatles were not especially thrilled with his lack of experience or the twenty-five percent he was asking for his services. But they needed someone to extend their careers beyond Liverpool and the Cavern. So they signed.

Epstein's plans for the Beatles were simple. He vowed to make them *bigger than Elvis,* and thus became the only manager in music business history to make good on that promise. He tried to clean up their scruffy image and put their financial affairs in order. But most of his time was spent trying to put together a record deal. A representative from Decca Records heard the group at the Cavern and set up an audition in the company's London studios. But after months of waiting, they were turned down. Brian was told that guitar groups were on the way out and advised to stick with his record store in Liverpool. But he was not discouraged. He continued to knock on doors, trying his best to convince record companies that he had England's first potential international superstars. After several more months of rejections, Epstein was finally referred to George Martin, a staff producer at EMI Records. Martin told writer Tony Palmer how it all started for him:

> I was looking for something new. I didn't know what I was looking for. Then Epstein walked into a recording company to get some [discs] cut of some of the Beatles tapes. The engineer thought they were interesting and telephoned a colleague of mine in the publishing branch. He called me and said: "This guy has been around every record company in London and he's getting nowhere. Will you see him? So I did. And as I listened to the tapes, I understood why everybody had turned them down — they were awful. But I asked Epstein to send the boys down for a test. When I met them I thought they were great. I didn't think their songs were very good. But I offered them a contract.

This was the break that the Beatles had been waiting for. Unfortunately though it meant the end for Pete Best. John, Paul, and George had already hired another drummer to take his place. The new man was Ringo Starr, who had worked at many of the same clubs in Liverpool and Hamburg with another "beat" group — Rory Storm and the Hurricanes. The reason for Best's firing has never been made clear. Apparently, the others felt that Ringo was a better drummer, and his image was right for them. Whatever the reasons, it must have been painful for poor Pete Best to have struggled all this time, only to be dumped when the group was on the verge of superstardom. Of the

Recording in London during the early 1960's
Record World—Capitol Records

hundreds of hirings and firings that have gone down in bands all over the world, the canning of Pete Best is particularly tragic. It is to his credit that he never accepted the many lucrative offers he had from magazines to reveal personal information about the Beatles.

In spite of the sadness caused by the Pete Best firing, there was one positive result. Ringo turned out to be the perfect complement to the Beatles — both musically and personally. While Pete always seemed a little out of place, Ringo quickly became as much a part of the Beatles' image as any of the others. Ironically, when the group finally made their first real record, George Martin chose a studio musician to play drums, and handed Ringo a pair of maracas. As it turned out though, the version of "Love Me Do" that was released had Ringo on drums. From that point on, Ringo was the only drummer to play on the Beatles records. Other musicians sometimes made guest appearances on their sessions, but the final Beatle lineup was set: John — vocals, rhythm guitar (harmonica, keyboards); Paul — vocals, bass guitar (acoustic guitar, keyboards); George — lead guitar, vocals; and Ringo — drums, occasional vocals.

BEATLE MADNESS

AFTER THE Beatles' second single — "Please Please Me" — made number one in England, the crowds at their performances began to go wild. Kids waited up to thirty-six hours in line to buy tickets. Once in the theatre, the noise was so loud that the Beatles couldn't hear themselves play. All sorts of manipulations were needed to get them out of the theatre and back to their hotel safely. Even Brian Epstein never anticipated such a hysterical response to his group. Wherever they performed, the scene was one of madness and bedlam. Throughout Europe, fans were wearing Beatle haircuts and breaking through police barricades in order to touch their heroes. At the end of 1963, the group was invited to play for the Royal Variety Performance. The concert was attended by the Queen Mother, Princess Margaret, Lord Snowden, and other prominent people. On this occasion, John delivered one of his most classic lines. After asking the audience to clap in time, he looked toward the royal box and said: "The rest of you just rattle your jewelry."

There were newsclips in America showing the pandemonium that the Beatles were causing in England, but no one was taking them very seriously. After all, no English performers had ever become big in the States. Suddenly, "I Want to Hold Your Hand," exploded to number one on the American charts, followed by "She Loves You." The American press began to take notice. Epstein responded by booking several key dates in America, including consecutive Sunday night appearances on the Ed Sullivan show.

The crowd's reaction on the Sullivan show kicked off Beatlemania in the United States. At first, it was only the young people who embraced the group. Many of the same intellectuals who were later to call them "the greatest musical talents of the twentieth century," were appalled by their early records. Here is a typical negative review that appeared in *The New Republic* in 1964:

> The Beatles are a semi-pro group out of Liverpool said to be worth seventeen million a year on the strength of their one act which arouses memories of the Nairobi Trio. The Nairobi Trio were three gorillas who used to appear on television playing one simple little tune over and over again. Occasionally one gorilla would peer mindlessly at another.

Taking a bow at New York's Shea Stadium
Record World—Capitol Records

For the next three years, the Beatles kept up a pace which rivaled their days in Hamburg. They traveled around the world, playing their twenty-five minute set for more people than any performers in history. In between these one-night stands, they found the time to go into the studio and record hit after hit. They also managed to make two feature films during that period — *A Hard Day's Night* and *Help.*

A Hard Day's Night depicted Beatlemania almost as it actually was. The film showed the boys performing for frantic audiences, escaping into a waiting car, sitting around joking in their hotel room, and talking to the press. Under the expert direction of Richard Lester, the Beatles made the greatest rock and roll comedy film of all time. They were all amazingly comfortable before the camera. John and Ringo both revealed real potential as actors.

Help was a high budget spoof of the spy films that were so popular at that time. Although it was less clever than *A Hard Day's Night*, this film was also quite funny and entertaining. The highlight of *Help*, though, was the music. In spite of their hectic touring schedule, the Beatles' sound was getting better all the time. The music in *Help* hinted at some of the new things the Beatles had in mind. John was showing a strong Bob Dylan influence on songs like "You Got To Hide Your Love Away," Paul was perfecting his ballad style, and George was becoming interested in Indian music.

In the Spring of 1966, the Beatles decided to stop performing live and devote all their time to making records. There were many reasons why they decided to stop touring, but mainly, they were just tired of it. "It was wrecking our playing," Ringo admitted to Hunter Davies. "The noise of the people just drowned anything. . . . I used to come in at the wrong time sometimes because I'd no idea where we were at. We just used to mime half the time to the songs, especially if your throat was feeling rough."

Some fans were so disappointed that the Beatles were no longer touring that they stopped buying their records. The three singles that came out after the announcement — "Paperback Writer," "Strawberry Fields Forever," and "Penny Lane," — were the first Beatles' records in years not to reach number one in England. However, it was immediately clear that the group was making groundbreaking advances in their music. Their next few albums would be so overwhelming that people would look back on this period as the golden era of Beatles' creativity.

Rubber Soul was the first Beatles' album to be made as a unified whole. Instead of consisting of a collection of twelve hit songs, *Rubber Soul* was truly an *album*. The songs were mostly about love, but a much more complex kind of love than in "I Want to Hold Your Hand." The music was less pounding than their earlier records, with many more subtle textures. There was a harpsichord solo in "In My Life," and a sitar on "Norwegian Wood." Ironically, the album's most uninspired song, "Michele," became one of the Beatles' most popular pieces. It was ballads like "Michele" and "Yesterday" that converted thousands of former rock 'n' roll haters into Beatle lovers.

Rubber Soul was a milestone for the Beatles in several ways. It was their first album which was regarded as "art," not simply good rock 'n' roll. For the first time, the group made specific references to their experiences with drugs. Looking back, *Rubber Soul* was the first indication that the Beatles were beginning to pursue their individual interests. Greil Marcus, writing in *The Rolling Stone Illustrated History of Rock and Roll*, illuminates these differences:

What was clear even on *Rubber Soul,* was that John and Paul were no longer the song-writing team they had once been. Consistently John's songs described struggle, while Paul's denied it; Paul wrote and sang the A sides, John the B's. Mapping out the directions that have governed their careers since the Beatles disbanded: John was already cultivating rebellion and anger; Paul was making his decision for pop; George was making his decision for Krishna; and Ringo was having his house painted.

The Beatles next album, *Revolver*, was more firmly rooted in the rock and R&B traditions than *Rubber Soul*. The differences between Lennon and McCartney styles were never more clear than on Paul's upbeat "Good Day Sunshine," and John's brooding "She Said She Said." In retrospect, *Revolver* may have been their best and most well-rounded album. Paul wrote "Eleanor Rigby," one of his most moving pieces, and "Got to Get You into My Life," one of his punchiest. Aside from his first recorded Indian-style song — "Love You To" — George also wrote and sang two solid rock songs — "Taxman," and "I Want to Tell You." Lennon wrote his most blatantly drug-oriented song, "Tomorrow Never Knows." And Ringo sang the album's hit single — the high spirited "Yellow Submarine." As great as *Rubber Soul* and *Revolver* were, it was a foregone conclusion that the Beatles' next album would be their masterpiece.

There was more anticipation preceding the *Sgt. Pepper's Lonely Hearts Club Band* than any record in history. The last two albums had taken rock music to its apex. Where could they possibly go from here? The Beatles had reached a point of total audience acceptance that was unmatched. They knew that anything they released would become a guaranteed commercial success. They decided to attempt to extend the traditional rock forms beyond all conventional boundaries. With the help of George Martin, they conceived of an album that had the scope of a film. The Beatles used a variety of electronic and musical devices ranging from harmonica quartets and animal noises to an entire classical orchestra. In order to create the impression of a unified theme, the Beatles discarded the traditional spaces between songs. Still, there is no real story line in the sense of The Who's rock opera *Tommy*. In fact, some of the songs seem to have no relation to any of the others. In retrospect, much of the album sounds contrived. There are a number of good songs, but only one real masterpiece — "A Day in the Life." On the basis of this song alone, *Sgt. Pepper* rates high on the list of rock's most important albums.

If hindsight reveals *Sgt. Pepper* to have been overrated at the time of its release, it is because so many critics were excessive with praise. One writer called the record, "the great contemporary bible." Lennon and McCartney's music was compared to Schumann and Beethoven, and John was said to be a poetic genius. Only one member of the rock press actually criticized *Sgt. Pepper*. Richard Goldstein of *The New York Times* agreed that "A Day in the Life" — "stands as one of the most important Lennon and McCartney compositions . . . an historic pop event." But for the most part, he found the album to be, "busy, hip, and cluttered . . . an elaboration without improvement." The Beatles themselves acted as if they couldn't understand why everybody was making such a fuss. "We never planned anything," Paul told Tony Palmer. "I still don't know what *Sgt. Pepper* was about. We always thought of ourselves as happy little songwriters just playing in a rock group."

But the Beatles weren't really such simple, happy people. For all their fame and fortune, life was often an emotional drain. They had experimented with marijuana and LSD. But now they felt it was time to give up drugs and seek spiritual peace from within. George was the first Beatle to become involved with meditation. Through him, the other members of the group got introduced to an Indian Guru — Maharishi Mahesh Yogi. Along with Mick Jagger and some other friends, the Beatles were initiated into Transcendental Med-

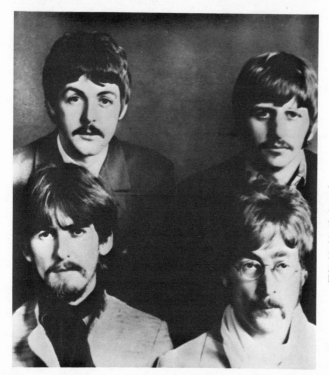

The Beatles in the
late 1960's—going
through changes
in their looks, and
in their minds.
Record World—Capitol
Records

itation. They returned to find that their manager, Brian Epstein, had died from an overdose of sleeping pills.

Epstein's death had a profound effect on the lives of the Beatles. He had always taken care of business matters and provided a buffer against the outside world. Now, they were on their own. "I was scared," John told Tony Palmer. "I thought: We've ... had it!" In fact, Epstein's death did signal the beginning of the end.

Shortly before their manager died, the Beatles had set up a new corporation — Apple. The company was set up in order to allow them to pursue their interests with complete creative freedom. They also announced plans to set up several foundations to help other artists. As John said at the time: "We want to set up a situation so people can make a film without getting down on their knees in somebody's office." There is no question that the Beatles had the best intentions going in. But without a real businessperson to run the show, things got out of hand. The Beatles put their friends in positions of power, and before long, millions of dollars had been squandered.

Nobody really expected the Beatles to be successful businessmen, but there were other problems. For the first time, their work was being harshly panned. Their initial project under the Apple umbrella was a made-for-TV film — *Magical Mystery Tour*. Unlike their first two movies, the Beatles decided to produce and direct this one themselves. The results were less than impressive, and the British press panned the film mercilessly. As if this wasn't bad enough, the group had to publicly admit that their recent trip to India with the Maharishi had also turned into a fiasco. Ringo was the first to leave, stating that he "didn't like the food." The rest followed in short order. The Beatles admitted that the Maharishi was "a mistake," althought they still retained their interest in meditation.

By the time the Beatles' first double album on Apple came out, it was apparent that the group was no longer a true merger of four talents. Instead, it was as if they were solo artists using the others as background musicians. The quality of the music, though, was excellent. *The Beatles* or "The White Album," as it has come to be called, holds up almost as well as *Rubber Soul* and *Revolver*. And if there was friction between various Beatles, the abundance of fine songs gave testimony to their strong individual talents. Paul and John were as good as ever. And George's "While My Guitar Gently Weeps," may be the best song he ever wrote.

Abbey Road, released in 1969, was still another case of John and the band, Paul and the band, and George and the band. If "The White Album" predicts the end of the Beatles and the idealistic visions of the sixties, *Abbey Road* is the group's last hurrah. Ringo had already tried to leave the group. He felt that his drum parts were being dictated by Paul and that he was given no creative freedom. George was having even worse problems with Paul. From the beginning, George had been given a supporting role. He received very little encouragement from the others on his songwriting. Apparently, John did not participate in most of the hassles. He had already become romantically and musically involved with the conceptual artist Yoko Ono. Together, they formed a separate group — the Plastic Ono Band — and began releasing records.

John's involvement with Yoko might have been the single greatest cause for the breakup of the Beatles. Her constant presence at recording sessions and her strong influence on John caused an imbalance in the group. Soon Paul got involved with Linda Eastman, and the stage was set for a full-scale war.

If the group's problems could have been restricted to musical matters, things might have been worked out. Even the personal friction caused by the John & Yoko vs. Paul & Linda situation might have eventually been resolved. But when the two wives became involved in the group's complex financial problems, the situation simply exploded. The Beatles had taken a severe beating with many of their Apple projects, and they needed someone to restore order to their deteriorating financial situation. Lennon wanted to hire New York accountant Allen Klein, who had also been involved with The Rolling Stones' management. But Paul didn't want Klein. He had married into a family of music-business lawyers, and the other Beatles suspected that Paul wanted to turn Apple over to them. By the time the dust settled, Paul was in court suing Klein and the other Beatles for a dissolution of their partnership.

The Beatles' last official project was the film *Let It Be*. Whatever its faults, the movie does document the group's breakup. There is footage of Paul and George arguing in the studio, and a number of other revealing scenes. The film ends with the group setting up on the roof of the Apple building and performing for the passersby on the street. The songs they played — "Get Back," "Don't Let Me Down," and several others — indicated that they were trying to return to their musical roots. Paul had been trying to encourage the others to get back into live performing. But this rooftop session in *Let It Be* was as close as they would come. The sixties were a part of the past, and so too were the Beatles.

THE DREAM ENDS

IN DISCUSSING the group's breakup, none of the Beatles have ever expressed surprise. They probably never envisioned that it would come to lawsuits and court injunctions, but they all knew that it had to come to an end sometime. When John Lennon said that the "dream is over," he wasn't only talking about the Beatles. He was also talking about the end of an era:

> We were all part of it. It happened to all of us. I feel just the same as everybody who was affected by it. Except somehow I was supposed to be separate. And I wasn't. I was just part of it. It does tend to put your image separate though. Or it makes people's idea of what you are separate. But I just went through it along with the other millions, and here we are now. . . .

In many ways, the Beatles breakup was the inevitable result of growing up. As their former press representative, Derek Taylor told *Newsweek* at the time: "It was easier for four boys to get together than four men with wives." They have all settled into their individual lives, and there is no longer any bitterness between them. But time has shown that the Beatles needed each other to make great music. On their own, they have all made some good records, some not-so-good records that sold well, and some flops. But even at their best as solo performers, there have been no *Rubber Souls*, no *Revolvers*, and no *Abbey Roads*.

PAUL MCCARTNEY

OF ALL THE ex-Beatles, Paul is the most successful and the most visible. He recently received an award for becoming the only songwriter in history to have written forty-three million-selling songs. He also owns many other publishing copyrights, including the entire Buddy Holly catalogue. In 1979, he signed a contract with Columbia Records which is reported to be the most lucrative ever given to any artist. As

Paul McCartney and Wings
Record World—Capitol Records

leader of the group Wings, Paul has been able to churn out hit after hit. Nobody can challenge his tremendous talent and creativity. But except for *Band on the Run* and a few other gems, Paul's music is nothing more than slick commercial product. He has sold a staggering total of 200 million records, and there is no reason to think that he won't keep this pace up.

Ever since the group's breakup, Paul has emphasized the importance of his family life. He and Linda spend much of their time on a sprawling farm in Scotland raising their children and living a rural life. In many ways, Paul seems the same as he did back in the early days. He is articulate, witty, and conveys the sense that he knows exactly what he is doing. He has also lost none of his considerable abilities as a singer and musician. Nevertheless, some of the magic he had as a Beatle has disappeared. One of the things that has hurt his credibility among many musicians is the inclusion of Linda in his band. It's very nice to know that he's happily married and loves his wife, but Linda simply is not a good musician. Would a great artist allow *his* wife to paint a few brush strokes on the canvas? Paul may be the most musically talented of all the ex-Beatles. But without Lennon's low harmonies and cynical personality, he has lost much of his creative bite.

GEORGE HARRISON

IF PAUL was the cutest and most ambitious Beatle, George was the most serious. He was the first to seek spiritual enlightenment, and he influenced the others to do the same. On the surface, it appeared that George had the most to gain by becoming a solo artist. He had come into his own as a writer during the late 1960's, though he was only usually allowed one or two songs per album. For the first two years after the breakup, George was the most active of all the ex-Beatles. His first solo album was a three-record set called *All Things Must Pass*. The album made it to number one, and showed that George really was a strong artist on his own. In 1971, he got Bob Dylan, Eric Clapton, Leon Russell and others to join him in a fund raising concert for the starving people of Bangladesh. This was a fine gesture on George's part, but it was undermined by a number of businessmen who prevented much of the money from ever reaching its charitable destination.

After that, George had a number of problems. First he was sued for using the music from another song on his hit single, "My Sweet Lord." Then, a 1974 tour of America proved disappointing. One of the problems was that George

George Harrison sits at the feet of his mentor—Indian sitar guru, Ravi Shankar.
Record World—Dark Horse Records

refused to respond to the crowds' demands for Beatles' songs. More than any of the others, George wanted to forget about his years as a Beatle. He is still very much involved with Eastern religion, though he usually avoids these influences in his music. His most recent album — *George Harrison* — is pleasant, but not great. He has no intentions of touring, and this probably is for the best. George lacks both the vocal ability and the inclination to be a frontman. In many ways, his role in the Beatles suited his talents quite well. But George has few regrets. The world of a rock star always meant less to him than to any of the others.

RINGO STARR

Ringo never had any illusions about his musical talent, or his role in the Beatles. While they were performing, he was as important as any of them. But when they became strictly a studio band, Ringo's role was greatly reduced. For the most part, Paul and John ran the show in the studio. Ringo often had to sit around for days with nothing to do, waiting until they were ready for him. Even then, his part was usually dictated to him by Paul. "I do sometimes feel out of it, sitting there on the drums, only playing what they tell me to play," Ringo told Hunter Davies. "Often when other drummers of groups say to me that was great, that bit, I know the others have usually told me what to do, though I've got the credit."

After the breakup, Ringo was the most tentative about pursuing a solo career. His singing voice had only been used as an occasional novelty by the Beatles. But his success on songs like "Yellow Submarine," and "With a Little Help from My Friends," showed that he could do the job when given the right piece of material. One of his albums, *Ringo*, made it to number two, and the follow-up *Goodnight Vienna*, also placed in the top ten. However, his career tapered off during the late seventies, and his albums did not create much excitement.

Today, Ringo lives the life of a jet-setter. Aside from his notoriety as a Beatle, he has appeared in several films over the years including, *Candy*, *The Magic Christian*, and Frank Zappa's *200 Motels*. Ringo spends much time in Monte Carlo, when he is not at his Los Angeles home. He enjoys being a celebrity far more than any of the other ex-Beatles. He always had a reputation for being the friendliest and the most easygoing of the four. As the least talented member of the group, he probably gained the most by being a Beatle.

"It'll be nice to be a part of history," Ringo told Hunter Davies. "What I'd like to be is in school history books and be read by kids."

JOHN LENNON

FROM THE beginning, John personified the Beatles more than any of the others. He was the most intellectual, and the most innovative. Though he wasn't as good a musician as George and Paul, John was probably the most original singer and the most creative songwriter. He was also the first to become bored with being a Beatle. Insiders agree that John's attitude toward the group changed when he became involved with Yoko Ono. The others resented that she was *always* around during the *Let It Be* sessions. There were many internal problems around that time, and it is likely that the group would have broken up anyway. But as John became more absorbed in Yoko, both artistically and emotionally, it became clear that the Beatles were doomed. With John disinterested, and Paul feuding with the others, there was no longer a sense of common purpose.

During the first few years after the breakup, John took most of the headlines. On his first album with Yoko — *Two Virgins* — both John and his bride posed nude. During this period, John, Yoko, and the Plastic Ono Band released political songs like "Give Peace a Chance," and "Power To The People." When John decided to become an American citizen in 1972, the U.S. Immigration Service attempted to deport him. Although the department based its case on a marijuana conviction in England in 1968, supporters of the Lennons felt certain that this was just an excuse to get rid of John and his outspoken politics. After several anxious years, John finally won his case and was allowed to remain.

John and Yoko also spent some time in primal therapy with Dr. Arthur Janov. His book, *The Primal Scream*, de-

John Lennon—Even more than his music, his humanity will be missed.
Record World—Capitol Records

scribed a method of psychotherapy by which one could ease his problems through crying and screaming. After this experience, John recorded a solo album — *John Lennon* — in which he attempted to release a lifetime of pent-up feelings. Although these confessions were unusually moving, they seemed a bit contrived. He did record a few gems during the early 1970's, most notably *Imagine*. But on the whole, Yoko's influence has not done anything for the quality of his music. Still, John credits his wife with changing his outlook: "Yoko's not just a lover and wife," he told *Record World.* "It's also mentally. She opened a part of my life that wasn't opened. Whether it would have happened without her, I don't know."

During the second half of the 70's, John dropped out of the music scene completely. Yoko began handling all of their business affairs, while John concentrated his energies on raising Sean—the couple's newborn baby boy. Other former Beatles were making hit records or mingling with the jet-set around the world, while John was busy changing Sean's diapers and fixing dinner. John had grown up never knowing his real father. So he wanted to provide a strong and loving presence for his own son.

After five years without a record, John and Yoko released

a new album, *Double Fantasy*. There were some pleasant cuts by John and a few surprisingly interesting songs by Yoko. This surely was not Lennon at his best. But it was good to have him back.

Double Fantasy had just come out. We were just beginning to hear songs like "Starting Over" on the radio. For the first time in years, John and Yoko were giving interviews. And even if they sounded as if they were trying to teach the world how men and women ought to relate, John seemed happier than ever. Then came the tragic night of December 8, 1980. A young man, apparently mentally disturbed and armed with a gun, waited for John in a dark corridor outside the Dakota, the famous building on New York's upper west side where the Lennons lived.

All assassinations are tragic. But the senseless killing of John Lennon is especially sad. Politicians know that they must protect themselves from potential assassins. But is this now also true of any person in the public eye? John Lennon chose to live in New York because it was a place where people left him alone. He and Yoko walked the streets with no bodyguards. They ate in local restaurants and mixed freely with people. For John Lennon was a man who treated people well. He was someone who cared about changing the world for the better and working for the things he believed in. That is why his needless killing is an even greater tragedy. Goodbye John! You will be missed.

BEATLES COLLECTORS' GUIDE
*— Smash Hit

ALBUMS

Year	Album	Label	Hit
1962	*Introducing the Beatles*	Vee-Jay	*

ALBUMS

Year	Album	Label	Hit
1964	Meet the Beatles	Capitol	*
1964	Beatles' Second Album	Capitol	*
1964	A Hard Day's Night	United Artists	*
1964	Something New	Capitol	*
1964	The Beatles' Story	Capitol	*
1965	Beatles '65	Capitol	*
1965	The Early Beatles	Capitol	
1965	Beatles VI	Capitol	*
1965	Help	Capitol	*
1965	Rubber Soul	Capitol	*
1966	Yesterday . . . and Today	Capitol	*
1966	Revolver	Capitol	*
1967	Sgt. Pepper's Lonely Hearts Club Band	Capitol	*
1967	Magical Mystery Tour	Capitol	*
1968	The Beatles ("White Album")	Apple	*
1969	Yellow Submarine	Apple	*
1969	Abbey Road	Apple	*
1970	Hey Jude	Apple	*
1970	Let It Be	Apple	*
1973	The Beatles 1962–66	Apple	*
1973	The Beatles 1967–70	Apple	*
1976	Rock 'n' Roll Music	Apple	*
1977	The Beatles at the Hollywood Bowl	Apple	*
1977	Love Songs	Apple	*
1980	Rarities	Capitol	*

SINGLES

Year	Single	Label	Hit
1964	I Want to Hold Your Hand	Capitol	*
1964	She Loves You	Swan	*
1964	Please Please Me	Vee-Jay	*

SINGLES

Year	Single	Label	Hit
1964	My Bonnie (w/Tony Sheridan)	MGM	
1964	I Saw Her Standing There	Capitol	*
1964	From Me to You	Vee-Jay	
1964	Twist and Shout	Tollie	*
1964	Roll Over Beethoven	Capitol of Canada	
1964	Can't Buy Me Love	Capitol	*
1964	Do You Want to Know a Secret	Vee-Jay	*
1964	All My Loving	Capitol of Canada	
1964	You Can't Do That	Capitol	
1964	Thank You Girl	Vee-Jay	
1964	Love Me Do	Tollie	*
1964	Why (w/Tony Sheridan)	MGM	
1964	P.S. I Love You	Tollie	*
1964	Four by the Beatles	Capitol	
1964	Sie Liebt Dich (She Loves You)	Swan	
1964	Ain't She Sweet	Atco	*
1964	A Hard Day's Night	Capitol	*
1964	I Should Have Known Better	Capitol	
1964	And I Love Her	Capitol	*
1964	If I Fell	Capitol	
1964	I'll Cry Instead	Capitol	
1964	I'm Happy Just to Dance with You	Capitol	
1964	Matchbox	Capitol	*
1964	Slow Down	Capitol	
1964	I Feel Fine	Capitol	*
1964	She's a Woman	Capitol	*
1965	8 Days a Week	Capitol	*
1965	I Don't Want to Spoil the Party	Capitol	
1965	Ticket to Ride	Capitol	*
1965	Yes It Is	Capitol	
1965	Help	Capitol	*
1965	Yesterday	Capitol	*

SINGLES

Year	Single	Label	Hit
1965	*Act Naturally*	Capitol	
1965	*We Can Work It Out*	Capitol	*
1965	*Day Tripper*	Capitol	*
1966	*Nowhere Man*	Capitol	*
1966	*What Goes On*	Capitol	
1966	*Paperback Writer*	Capitol	*
1966	*Rain*	Capitol	
1966	*Yellow Submarine*	Capitol	*
1966	*Eleanor Rigby*	Capitol	*
1967	*Penny Lane*	Capitol	*
1967	*Strawberry Fields Forever*	Capitol	*
1967	*All You Need Is Love*	Capitol	*
1967	*Baby You're a Rich Man*	Capitol	
1967	*Hello Goodbye*	Capitol	*
1967	*I Am the Walrus*	Capitol	
1968	*Lady Madonna*	Capitol	*
1968	*The Inner Light*	Capitol	
1968	*Hey Jude*	Apple	*
1968	*Revolution*	Apple	*
1969	*Get Back (w/Billy Preston)*	Apple	*
1969	*Don't Let Me Down*	Apple	
1969	*The Ballad of John and Yoko*	Apple	*
1969	*Come Together*	Apple	*
1970	*Let It Be*	Apple	*
1970	*The Long and Winding Road*	Apple	*
1970	*For You Blue*	Apple	
1976	*Got to Get You into My Life/Helter Skelter*	Capitol	*
1976	*Ob-La-Di, Ob-La-Da*	Capitol	

PAUL McCARTNEY COLLECTORS' GUIDE
* — *Smash Hit*

ALBUMS

Year	Album	Label	Hit
1970	McCartney (w/Linda McCartney)	Apple	*
1971	Ram (w/Linda McCartney)	Apple	*
1971	Wild Life (w/Wings)	Apple	*
1973	Red Rose Speedway (w/Wings)	Apple	*
1973	Band on the Run (w/Wings)	Apple	*
1975	Venus and Mars (w/Wings)	Capitol	*
1976	Wings at the Speed of Sound (w/Wings)	Capitol	*
1976	Wings Over America (w/Wings)	Capitol	*
1978	Wings Greatest Hits (w/Wings)	Capitol	*
1978	London Town (w/Wings)	Capitol	*
1979	Back to the Egg (w/Wings)	Columbia	*
1980	McCartney II	Columbia	*

SINGLES

Year	Single	Label	Hit
1971	Another Day	Apple	*
1971	Uncle Albert-Admiral Halsey (w/Linda McCartney)	Apple	*
1972	Give Ireland Back to the Irish (w/Wings)	Apple	
1972	Mary Had a Little Lamb (w/Wings)	Apple	
1972	Hi, Hi, Hi (w/Wings)	Apple	*
1973	My Love (w/Wings)	Apple	*
1973	Live and Let Die (w/Wings)	Apple	*

SINGLES

Year	Single	Label	Hit
1973	Helen Wheels (w/Wings)	Apple	
1974	Jet (w/Wings)	Apple	*
1974	Band on the Run (w/Wings)	Apple	*
1974	Walking in the Park with Eloise (by Wings and the Country Hams)	Apple	
1974	Junior's Farm (w/Wings)	Apple	*
1975	Listen to What the Man Said (w/Wings)	Capitol	*
1975	Venus and Mars Rock Show (w/Wings)	Capitol	*
1975	Letting Go (w/Wings)	Capitol	
1976	Silly Love Songs (w/Wings)	Capitol	*
1976	Let 'Em In (w/Wings)	Capitol	*
1977	Maybe I'm Amazed (w/Wings)	Capitol	*
1977	Girls' School (w/Wings)	Capitol	
1978	With a Little Bit of Luck (w/Wings)	Capitol	*
1979	Goodnight Tonight (w/Wings)	Columbia	*
1979	Getting Closer (w/Wings)	Columbia	*
1979	Arrow through Me (w/Wings)	Columbia	*
1980	Coming Up	Columbia	*

JOHN LENNON COLLECTORS' GUIDE

* — Smash Hit

ALBUMS

Year	Album	Label	Hit
1968	2 Virgins (Tetragrammaton)	Apple	
1969	Unfinished Music No. 2: Life with the Lions (w/Yoko Ono)	Zapple	

ALBUMS

Year	Album	Label	Hit
1969	*Wedding Album (w/Yoko Ono)*	Apple	
1970	*The Plastic Ono Band Live Peace in Toronto (w/The Plastic Ono Band)*	Apple	*
1970	*Plastic Ono Band*	Apple	*
1971	*Imagine*	Apple	*
1972	*Sometime in New York City (w/Yoko Ono, Elephants Memory and Invisible Strings)*	Apple	
1973	*Mind Games*	Apple	*
1974	*Walls and Bridges*	Apple	*
1975	*Rock 'n' Roll*	Apple	*
1975	*Shaved Fish*	Apple	*
1980	*Double Fantasy*	Geffen	*

SINGLES

Year	Single	Label	Hit
1969	*Give Peace a Chance*	Apple	*
1969	*Cold Turkey (w/Plastic Ono Band)*	Apple	*
1970	*Instant Karma (w/Yoko Ono and the Plastic Ono Band)*	Apple	*
1971	*Mother (w/Yoko Ono and the Plastic Ono Band)*	Apple	
1971	*Power to the People (w/Yoko Ono and the Plastic Ono Band)*	Apple	*
1971	*God Save Us (w/the Elastic Oz Band)*	Apple	
1971	*Happy Xmas (War Is Over) (w/Yoko Ono and the Plastic Ono Band and the Harlem Community Choir)*	Apple	*
1972	*Woman Is the Nigger of the World (w/The Plastic Ono Band, Elephants Memory and the Invisible Strings)*	Apple	
1973	*Mind Games*	Apple	*

SINGLES

Year	Single	Label	Hit
1974	Whatever Gets You thru the Night (w/The Plastic Ono Nuclear Band)	Apple	
1974	#9 Dream	Apple	
1975	Stand By Me	Apple	*

GEORGE HARRISON COLLECTORS' GUIDE
— Smash Hit

ALBUMS

Year	Album	Label	Hit
1969	Wonderwall	Apple	
1969	Electronic Sound	Zapple	
1970	All Things Must Pass	Apple	*
1972	The Concert for Bangla Desh (w/friends)	Apple	*
1973	Living in the Material World	Apple	*
1974	Dark Horse	Apple	*
1975	Extra Texture (Read All About It)	Apple	*
1976	The Best of George Harrison	Apple	
1976	33⅓	Dark Horse	
1979	George Harrison	Dark Horse	

SINGLES

Year	Single	Label	Hit
1970	My Sweet Lord/Isn't It a Pity	Apple	*
1971	What Is Life/Apple Scruffs	Apple	*
1971	Bangla Desh/Deep Blue	Apple	*
1973	Give Me Love (Give Me Peace on Earth)/Miss O'Dell	Apple	*

SINGLES

Year	Single	Label	Hit
1974	*Dark Horse/I Don't Care Any More*	Apple	*
1974	*Ding Dong; Ding Dong/Hari's on Tour*	Apple	
1975	*You/World of Stone*	Apple	*
1975	*This Guitar Can't Keep From Crying*	Apple	
1976	*This Song/Learning How to Love You*	Dark Horse	
1976	*Crackerbox Palace/Beautiful Girls*	Dark Horse	
1979	*Blow Away*	Dark Horse	

RINGO STARR COLLECTORS' GUIDE
*— Smash Hit

ALBUMS

Year	Album	Label	Hit
1970	*Sentimental Journey*	Apple	
1970	*Beaucoups of Blues*	Apple	
1973	*Ringo*	Apple	*
1974	*Goodnight Vienna*	Apple	*
1975	*Blast from Your Past*	Apple	
1976	*Ringo Rotogravure*	Apple	
1977	*Richard the 4th*	Atlantic	
1979	*Bad*	Portrait	

SINGLES

Year	Single	Label	Hit
1970	*Beaucoups of Blues*	Apple	
1971	*It Don't Come Easy*	Apple	*
1972	*Back off Boogaloo*	Apple	*

SINGLES

Year	Single	Label	Hit
1973	*Photograph*	Apple	*
1973	*You're Sixteen*	Apple	*
1974	*Oh My My*	Apple	*
1974	*Only You*	Apple	*
1975	*Snookeroo/No No Song*	Apple	*
1975	*It's All down to Goodnight Vienna*	Apple	
1976	*Hey Baby*	Portrait	
1976	*Dose of Rock 'n' Roll*	Portrait	
1978	*Lipstick Traces (on a Cigarette)*	Portrait	

Supergroups

3. THE ROLLING STONES

ALL THINGS considered, The Rolling Stones symbolize rock
'n' roll more than any other contemporary performers. The
group was formed in 1962 and became the first of many English bands to follow the Beatles on the road to international
success. But while most of these bands — including the
Beatles — have been defunct for years, the Stones are still at
the top of their field. As they enter their third decade as a
recording and performing band, The Rolling Stones remain
as vital as ever. It is not only their sound that has been copied by thousands of other bands, but also their look and
lifestyle.

The most well-known Rolling Stone by far is lead singer
Mick Jagger. One of the truly great rock performers of all
time, Jagger has become one of the most well recognized
superstars in the world. His uninhibited stage presence has
become the model for countless others, and his personal

exploits make the headlines of newspapers and magazines all over the world. But Mick Jagger is a man of many talents; he is the co-writer of virtually all the Stones' songs, a number of which rank among the greatest rock tunes ever written, and he is a talented actor who gave a riveting performance as a violent, egotistical, and bisexual rock star in the 1970 film *Performance*. Jagger is also a highly intelligent person. Many insiders claim that he is the brains behind the Stones' success. But first and foremost, Mick's main concern has always been the group's music.

During the late 1950's, Mick had developed a keen interest in the music of authentic blues performers such as Elmore James and Muddy Waters. He had done some singing with local groups and hoped someday to become a full-time performer. In the meantime, however, Mick enrolled in the London School of Economics. He was not yet ready to devote himself completely to music. One day, while taking the train to school, Mick ran into an old boyhood chum, Keith

Mick Jagger—"Sexually satisfied, financially dissatisfied, and philosophically trying."
Record World—Rolling Stones Records

Richards. The two had grown up in the same working-class suburb of London, but lost touch when Keith's family moved into a housing project in another part of town. By this time, Keith had enrolled in art school, where he had begun to experiment with the guitar.

Both boys were part of a growing number of British teenagers who had become interested in authentic rock 'n' roll, and blues records. In fact, Jagger was carrying a number of these records under his arm that day on the train. When Keith realized that Mick shared his passion for artists like Chuck Berry and Little Richard, he suggested that they get together.

A short time later, Mick and Keith began spending a great deal of time listening to records and jamming with some other young musicians. One night, they went to a local rhythm and blues club where the English blues musician Alexis Korner was performing. At the beginning of his second set, Korner introduced a young guitarist from Cheltenham who had come to sit in with the band. The guitarist was Brian Jones, and it was clear by his playing that he had been listening to the same blues records as Mick and Keith. Although Brian was more advanced musically than the other two, he sensed that a common ground existed and agreed to cast his lot with them. The three young men rented an apartment in the Chelsea section of London in order to have a place to pursue their musical ambitions.

The nucleus of The Rolling Stones was now assembled. The three rehearsed constantly, and the music began falling into place. But the group lacked the two musicians who provide the pulse of any rock 'n' roll band — a bass player and a drummer. Within a short time though, they hooked up with a bassist named Bill Wyman.

In an interview with the English magazine *New Musical Express*, Wyman told of his early days with the band: "They didn't like me, but I had a good amplifier, and they were badly in need of amplifiers at that time! So they kept me on. Later when they were going to get rid of me, I think I clicked or something, and I stayed. I must have fitted in." Apparently, Wyman fit in quite well since he is the only bass player the Stones have ever had.

The group worked for several months without a full-time drummer. One night Charlie Watts, who played drums for another band, heard the Stones and liked what he heard. Watts had been working a day job and playing drums with semi-pro bands on weekends. Within a short time, he gave up his other interests and became a full-time Stone.

The Rolling Stones' lineup was now complete. They soon began working at London's Crawdaddy Club and became the city's top band. In April 1963, Andrew Oldham, an aspiring manager, signed the group and promptly got them a record contract with British Decca. By June, their first single — "Come On" — was on the British charts. The Stones also appeared on television and were written up in a number of British newspapers.

Before the year was out, the band toured England on a bill which also included Bo Diddley, and the Everly Brothers. They also placed a second single — "I Want to be Your Man" — on the British Hit Parade. The song was written by Beatles John Lennon and Paul McCartney. Its success inspired Jagger and Richards to start writing their own original material.

By 1964, the Stones were touring as the headline act. Their records were starting to create excitement in the United States, and in June they embarked on their first American tour. Since they were only the second British group to become popular in the States, the Stones were constantly subjected to comparisons with their forerunners, the Beatles. In fact, the Stones seemed to spend their first five years chasing the Beatles.

In terms of personal and musical history, the two groups

did have some things in common. They were both inspired by early rock 'n' rollers like Chuck Berry, Buddy Holly, and Little Richard. Both bands started out playing familiar rock 'n' roll songs in clubs and eventually moved to their own original material. For the most part, the members of both groups came from working-class families. In spite of these similarities, however, the Beatles and the Stones came to represent completely different outlooks and sensibilities.

From the beginning, the Stones' sound was tougher and more sexual than the Beatles. While Lennon and McCartney went for a more high-pitched, innocent vocal sound, Jagger patterned his vocals after the rougher tones of country blues performers. The Beatles used many background harmonies and catchy words, while the Stones wrote words that were more direct and depended mostly on Jagger's lead voice. These musical differences also related to the personal styles and attitudes of the members of the two groups.

In contrast to the Beatles — who had a public image of being cute, witty, and relatively cleancut — the Stones looked unkempt and were often impolite, especially at press conferences. At first, their manager tried to get them to clean up their act. But soon even he stopped trying.

The Stones were really dressing and acting naturally. But they quickly began to use this negative image to their advantage. Of course, the press played right into their hands by running stories like these:

May 27, 1964 — *The headmaster of a British school says boys may cut their hair in the style of the Beatles, but not like Mick Jagger. Several days later, eleven boys with Jagger-type haircuts are suspended.*

July 1, 1965 — *Three members of The Rolling Stones are fined five pounds each for insulting the owner of a filling station.*

Aside from all the help that they got from the press, the Stones have done much to fuel their own outrageous image.

Many of their song lyrics are simply too explicit to be played on many AM radio stations. Thus, many of their records are mixed so that the instrumental track drowns out the lyrics.

In terms of their behavior, the Stones have enjoyed "blowing people's minds." For example, they have shown a decided preference for dressing up as women for record jacket photographs. Most of the group's fans find this amusing. But the Stones enjoy knowing that certain people will be shocked by such behavior. Jagger and friends take delight in offending people who dislike their tough, street-wise attitude. In spite of all their drug busts and other exploits — both real and fictitious — their lasting influence has little to do with their offbeat personalities.

The fact remains that Jagger and Richards have written some of the greatest rock 'n' roll songs of all time, and the Stones' versions of these songs tower above all others. Their music is pure rock 'n' roll. It appeals only to people who love that particular kind of tough, simple music. The Stones never moved away from their original roots, although they did occasionally experiment with unusual musical instruments and forms. But unlike the Beatles, they never really made inroads into the mainstream of popular music. With a few notable exceptions, they did not go in for complex recording studio techniques. The Stones have always been a performing band, and this has tended to keep their work in the studio closer to what can be performed live.

Since the death of Brian Jones in 1969, the group has had two rhythm guitarists, Mick Taylor from 1969 to 1974, and Ron Wood, from 1974 to the present. Otherwise, the personnel of the group has remained unchanged. Although the Stones have maintained a similar sound throughout their career, it is possible to pinpoint several distinct phases. Not surprisingly, these phases correspond roughly to the shifting of guitarists.

When the group first formed during the early sixties, Brian Jones was its most accomplished musician. During his years with the Stones, he played harmonica, sitar, and flute as well as guitar. His versatility was most helpful on the group's early records. But Brian had a number of personal problems which eventually made him unable to perform. Keith Richards, in a rare interview, told a reporter for *Rolling Stone* that Brian could not get along with him and Mick at the same time. Although Mick was always the dominant personality in the group, Brian felt that *he* should be getting more attention.

In reality, it takes a strong person to cope with being a rock star, and Brian just wasn't that strong. Playing a string of one-night stands and dealing with thousands of screaming fans who are sometimes ready to tear you apart physically is no easy chore. Brian reached a point where he was no longer able to cope. Eventually, his performance in the studio was affected as well. Richards recalled that on a number of Stones records, he was forced to overdub three guitar parts, while Brian was "zonked out on the floor."

In June of 1969, Brian left the group to "pursue his own music." One month later he was dead. The cause of his death was drowning, though no one has ever really explained how a good swimmer like Brian could drown in his own pool. He did have asthma and was often reckless in his use of drugs and alcohol, but the true cause of Brian's death is still shrouded in mystery.

Like a number of other rock stars who died prematurely, Brian did seem to have a self-destructive and reckless nature. As rock critic Greil Marcus pointed out: "Brian lived the life that the Stones sang about. His exploits with women resulted in paternity suits; he was the group's loudest dresser, and the first to get busted for grass." A writer for *Rolling Stone* put it best when he said: "If Mick and Keith were the mind and body of The Rolling Stones, Brian Jones,

Guitarist-songwriter
Keith Richards, a cult
figure in his own right.
Record World—Rolling Stones Records

standing most of the time in the shadows, was clearly its soul."

Many of the early Stones records during the Brian Jones era were loose and sloppy, and the fault did not always rest with Brian. In spite of the out-of-tune notes and missed beats which characterize the early cuts, this was rock 'n' roll with an energy that went beyond the music the Stones had been influenced by. It was soon clear that the group was moving away from rhythm and blues imitation and into its own style.

Ironically, the Stones' explorations into the work of the great blues musicians helped the latter to expand their audiences. Artists like Muddy Waters — whose song "Rolling Stone" inspired the group's name — suddenly found themselves working in front of large numbers of young, white rock fans. Previously, these musicians were popular mostly among black listeners.

Meanwhile, the Stones were coming into their own as stars in America. Their first number-one hit in the United States was "Satisfaction," in 1965. This record is considered by many to be the greatest pure rock 'n' roll song of all time. It was now clear that the Stones had created a distinct style of rock that took the work of authentic rockers like Chuck Berry a step further. The lyrics of the song seemed to work best when Jagger sang them, while cover versions by R&B greats like Otis Redding and Aretha Franklin often lost the impact of the originals.

During the next few years, the group turned out several fine albums, including *December's Children* and *Aftermath.* Both of these LP's contained a number of R&B remakes, but it was the Jagger-Richards originals that stood out. A number of these songs became hit singles such as: "Get Off My Cloud," "As Tears Go By," and "Mother's Little Helper."

In 1967, the Stones released their first album of completely original material — *Between the Buttons.* The group was now expanding its style even further, incorporating influences ranging all the way from Old English Ballads to Bob Dylan. The album contained the two-sided smash single "Ruby Tuesday," b/w "Let's Spend the Night Together." Although *Between the Buttons* is considered one of their best records from this period, Jagger has since expressed his dissatisfaction with it.

On their next album — *Their Satanic Majesties' Request* — the Stones presented their very own answer to the Beatles' *Sgt. Pepper* LP. From the extravagant cover art to the one-theme connecting of songs, the Stones seemed to be trying to out-Beatle the Beatles. *Satanic Majesties* was panned by most rock critics for being pretentious and excessive. Still, there were some good moments on the album. But this was not the kind of music that most Stones fans craved.

Fortunately, the Stones did not continue to pursue this

musical direction. Instead, they returned to basic rock 'n' roll on their next album — *Beggars Banquet*. Some of the songs even had a country twang, thanks to Brian's steel guitar playing. From this album came the classics, "Street Fighting Man" and "Sympathy for the Devil." *Beggars Banquet* represented a turning point for the Stones in several respects. It was Brian's last album with the group, and it was the first time Jimmy Miller had been employed as the band's producer.

The addition of Mick Taylor on guitar seemed to help the Stones' sound greatly. With producer Miller now at the controls, the group turned out some of its finest music. Taylor's playing seemed to click immediately with Keith's, and the band sounded tighter than ever. Songs like "Honky Tonk Women" and "Brown Sugar," featured crisp exchanges of riffs by the two guitarists. Miller tastefully added horns to these songs and cleaned up the sound without losing any of its intensity. Suddenly, the Stones had a professional, almost slick sound which they had lacked during their early years.

Shortly after Taylor joined the band, a month-long tour of the United States was planned. The tour was to end with a free concert for 300 thousand people at Altamont Park in San Francisco. The event was being billed as another Woodstock. It was hoped that the huge crowd would show the kind of cooperation and restraint that they had exhibited at the earlier festival.

Instead, the concert turned into a nightmare of bad drugs, inadequate facilities, needless violence, and death. The tension was obvious throughout the day, as members of the Hell's Angels motorcycle gang violently beat several spectators. The members of this notorious motorcycle club had been hired by the Stones as security guards in exchange for five-hundred-dollars' worth of beer. The Angels had often been used to keep order at free concerts, and it wasn't surprising that the Grateful Dead suggested that the Stones employ them for this purpose. The massive audience was pushing and shoving in order to get a better look at the stage, while performers like Jefferson Airplane's Grace Slick pleaded with the crowd to keep cool. But as the Stones started to play their long-awaited set, a young black man began waving a gun and was knifed to death, allegedly by a member of Hell's Angels. There were also two drug-related deaths at Altamont, but it was the violence there that signaled the end of the love era of the sixties.

The following year, the movie *Gimme Shelter* was released. The horrors of Altamont were shown for all to see, along with highlights from the rest of the tour. Suddenly, the violence that had always been a part of much of the Stones' music became painfully real. Perhaps they never should have hired the violence-prone Hell's Angels in exchange for beer. Perhaps they should have insisted on better security, or simply not performed at all. The Stones had never associated themselves with the peace movement or the hippie movement of the sixties. Perhaps they really believed that they had no responsibility to their audience. The questions raised by the tragedy at Altamont have never been answered by the Stones or anyone else. But a number of conservative writers considered the concert an end to the "flower power" era of the sixties.

In spite of the bad publicity caused by the events at Altamont, The Rolling Stones reached their commercial and artistic peak during the three years that followed. Their *Sticky Fingers* album was probably the best they had ever done. This was followed by another exceptional album, *Exile on Main Street*. But the group seemed to run out of steam around 1973. Their next two records, *Goat's Head Soup* and *It's Only Rock and Roll*, were well below par for them.

These two albums were to be Mick Taylor's last recordings with the Stones. Although he had the right sound and even the right look, Mick was rather shy, and did not seem comfortable as a Rolling Stone. His replacement, Ron Wood, appears to be much more relaxed in the role. Since Wood joined the band in 1975, Keith seems content to stay more in the background. To what extent this attitude reflects his personal problems is still unclear. One thing is certain: The Rolling Stones came out of their slump during the late seventies.

In the spring of 1978, the Stones released a new album, *Some Girls*, which re-established their position as the top group in rock. A number of songs from the album became hit singles, including: "Shattered," "Beast of Burden," and "Miss You." The latter song is notable in that it uses a disco beat without diluting the hard-edge rock sound of the Stones. Since the release of "Miss You," a number of other established rock performers have tried to make records

The Rolling Stones in concert (*left to right*) Ron Wood, Keith Richards, Charlie Watts, Bill Wyman.
Record World—Rolling Stones Records

with a disco beat. With one notable exception, Rod Stewart's "Do You Think I'm Sexy," most of these have missed the mark.

After the release of *Some Girls*, the Stones embarked on a tour of the United States and Canada. In addition to the huge arenas in which they normally performed, the group scheduled a number of bookings in smaller, more intimate halls. The tour was extremely well received by both fans and critics.

No true lover of rock 'n' roll would ever question how important the Stones have been. But as Jagger and the other original members approach their forties, one can only ask, how long will they be able to go on?

ROLLING STONES COLLECTORS' GUIDE
— Smash Hit

ALBUMS

Year	Album	Label	Hit
1964	The Rolling Stones	London	*
1964	12 × 15	London	*
1965	The Rolling Stones Now	London	*
1965	Out of Our Heads	London	*
1965	December's Children (And Everybody)	London	*
1966	Big Hits (High Tide and Green Grass)	London	*
1966	Aftermath	London	*
1966	Got "Live" If You Want It	London	*
1967	Between the Buttons	London	*
1967	Flowers	London	*
1967	Their Satanic Majesties Request	London	*
1968	Beggars Banquet	London	*

ALBUMS

Year	Album	Label	Hit
1969	Through the Past Darkly (Big Hits Volume II)	London	*
1969	Let It Bleed	London	*
1970	Get Yer Ya-Ya's Out	London	*
1971	Sticky Fingers	Rolling Stones	*
1972	Hot Rocks 1964–1971	London	*
1972	Exile on Main Street	Rolling Stones	*
1972	More Hot Rocks (Big Hits and Fazed Cookies)	London	*
1975	Made in the Shade	Rolling Stones	*
1976	Black and Blue	Rolling Stones	*
1977	Love You Live	Rolling Stones	*
1978	Some Girls	Rolling Stones	*
1980	Emotional Rescue	Rolling Stones	*

SINGLES

Year	Single	Label	Hit
1964	I Wanna Be Your Man	London	
1964	Not Fade Away	London	
1964	Tell Me (You're Coming Back to Me)/I Just Want to Make Love to You	London	
1964	It's All Over Now/Good Times, Bad Times	London	
1964	Time Is on My Side/Congratulations	London	*
1965	Heart of Stone/What a Shame	London	*
1965	The Last Time/Play with Fire	London	*
1965	Satisfaction/The Under Assistant West Coast Promotion Man	London	*
1965	Get off My Cloud/I'm Free	London	*
1965	As Tears Go By/Gotta Get Away	London	*
1966	19th Nervous Breakdown/Say Day	London	*
1966	Paint It Black/Stupid Girl	London	*

SINGLES

Year	Single	Label	Hit
1966	*Mother's Little Helper/Lady Jane*	London	*
1966	*Have You Seen Your Mother Baby Standing in the Shadow/Who's Driving My Plane*	London	*
1967	*Ruby Tuesday/Let's Spend the Night Together*	London	*
1967	*Dandelion/We Be You*	London	*
1967	*She's a Rainbow/2,000 Light Years from Home*	London	
1967	*In Another Land (written and sung by Bill Wyman)/The Lantern*	London	*
1968	*Jumpin' Jack Flash/Child of the Moon*	London	*
1969	*Honky Tonk Women/You Can't Always Get What You Want*	London	*
1971	*Brown Sugar*	Rolling Stones	*
1971	*Wild Horses*	Rolling Stones	
1972	*Tumbling Dice*	Rolling Stones	*
1972	*Happy*	Rolling Stones	
1973	*You Can't Always Get What You Want*	London	
1973	*Angie*	Rolling Stones	*
1974	*Doo Doo Doo Doo Doo (Heartbreaker)*	Rolling Stones	*
1974	*It's Only Rock and Roll (But I Like It)*	Rolling Stones	*
1974	*Ain't Too Proud to Beg*	Rolling Stones	*
1975	*I Don't Know Why/Out of Time*	Abkco	
1976	*Fool to Cry/Hot Stuff*	Rolling Stones	*
1978	*Miss You*	Rolling Stones	*
1978	*Shattered*	Rolling Stones	
1978	*Beast of Burden*	Rolling Stones	

Supergroups

4. THE BEE GEES

"There's always a link between brothers. This business doesn't split them up quite so much as another group of people making music." — Barry Gibb

THE BEE GEES have been making music for over a quarter of a century, and it shows. Their incredibly tight vocal sound could only come from brothers who have been singing together most of their lives. But Barry Gibb and his fraternal twin brothers, Robin and Maurice, have a tightness that goes beyond music. They are a family in the old-fashioned sense of the word. When the group goes on tour, the groupies and other hangers-on that usually attach themselves to rock stars are missing. Instead, the Bee Gees entourage often includes wives, children and parents.

Even if the brothers decide to split for a while to pursue individual record and film careers, they could always reunite. The Gibbs value the importance of family feeling and warmth in a business that is often cold and impersonal. But Barry, Maurice, and Robin are more than the pillars of a close-knit family. They are among the most successful per-

The Bee Gees—Robin, Barry, and Maurice Gibb
Record World—RSO Records

formers and songwriters in the history of popular music.

Long before their 1977 soundtrack of *Saturday Night Fever* became the best-selling album of all time, the Bee Gees were writing hit songs and making hit records. In fact, the brothers have been consistent hit-makers since 1967. Most of their records in the sixties were romantic ballads, and a number of them have become "standards." Their 1969 album, *The Best of the Bee Gees* contains great tunes like "To Love Somebody," "I Can't See Nobody," "Massachusetts," and "Words." This work alone would have assured the brothers a high place in the history of popular music, but it took another ten years for them to reach the peak of their great success.

When Maurice Gibb was recently asked what had changed most about the group during their twenty years as professionals, he sarcastically replied — "Our underwear, and me losing my hair." Well, this may be somewhat of an exaggeration. But in many respects, the Bee Gees aren't really that much different from the way they were ten or fifteen years ago. They have always displayed a rich and unique vocal sound, and an uncanny ability for writing hit songs.

"Even when we were little kids," Robin Gibb recalls, "we had a natural three-part harmony." By the time Barry was ten, and Robin, and Maurice were seven, they were singing professionally. The boys made their first public appearance in 1956, at the local movie theater in their hometown of Manchester, England. "We weren't actually singing on-stage," recalls Barry, who was nine at the time. "We were miming to records by people like Tommy Steele and Paul Anka at the cinema matinees. On the way to the theater, the record broke and we were forced to sing!" "The guy who was the manager just threw a microphone in front of us, and we sang 'Lollipop,' " Maurice adds. "We used to sing that song at home, but we never harmonized 'til we were on stage."

In 1958, the Gibb family moved to Australia. The boys' father, Hugh Gibb, had been struggling as a drummer and bandleader in the cold, industrial town of Manchester. Australia held all the promise of a wide-open new land with a warm climate to boot. The following year, the brothers started performing between races at the Redcliffe Speedway in Brisbane. The crowds were so knocked out by the youngsters' singing that they threw down a tidy sum of money when the hat was passed. The Gibb family was having financial problems during those years and sorely needed this cash that the boys were bringing home. "Singing wasn't a question of having a career at that point," Robin explains. "It was a question of survival."

A short time later, the brothers were taken under the wing of Bill Gates, a well-known Australian disc jockey. First he changed their name from the Rattlesnakes to the Bee Gees (short for the Brothers Gibb). Then he took the boys into a small studio behind a butcher shop and recorded several of Barry's original songs. Local response to their music was so great that Hugh Gibb felt his sons might have a real chance in the music business. Then in 1960, the boys landed their own thirty-minute television show. They also put together a live act and began playing the Australian nightclub circuit.

In 1963, the brothers signed a record deal with an Australian label — Fantasy. Their first single, "Three Kisses of Love," got some air play, but didn't really go anywhere. The group made a dozen more records during the next three years and finally got several of them on the Australian charts. In 1965–1966, the Bee Gees were voted the best songwriting team and vocal group in Australia. But by that time, they had decided to return to England.

It wasn't very difficult for the Gibbs to see that their horizons in Australia were limited. While the Beatles had brought England to the forefront of the international rock scene, the Bee Gees were unknown outside of their adopted land. But the brothers were certain that they had more going for them than most of the popular British invasion groups that were dominating the hit parade. They also knew that there wasn't likely to be any such thing as an "Australian invasion."

"Australian record companies need better links with the outside," notes Barry Gibb. "There's an enormous amount of talent there, but it never seems to get out with any regularity. Having a number-one record in Australia only means you can have a chance of having more there — and maybe a few in New Zealand. . . . Australia gave us basic training for the international market which we were always aiming for. So, we left for a market that wasn't so closed minded — England."

Almost immediately after they left Australia, one of their singles — "Spicks and Specks" — became the number-one record in that country. Finally, they had achieved total acceptance in their adopted land. They had become the biggest fish in a small pond. As much as they believed in their talent, the brothers were in no way assured of how they would be received in England. But as Hugh Gibb told *Record World*, the time was right for this kind of move.

> The thing about Australia is that it's such a big country, and there's a lot of interstate rivalry between cities like Sydney, Brisbane, and Melbourne. You can have a number-one hit in Sydney, but that doesn't mean a thing in Melbourne or Perth, which is nearly six thousand miles away. This happened for a period of time. But in late 1966 they had a number 1 nationally, all over Australia. This is quite an achievement there. Once they made it big in each state, that was it. . . . The boys wanted to come back to England. We arrived with seven hundred dollars, and didn't know what was going to happen. I mean if you've got to the top in Australia, you've got to go to England or the States.

Although 1967 was a time during which record companies were seeking out new talent, Barry recalls that the first words they heard upon arriving in London were discouraging. "When we first got there, a group of musicians we met who were sleeping at a train station said 'Go back, it's all *Cream!*' And we didn't even know then who *Cream* was."

Nevertheless, it didn't take the Bee Gees long to get hooked up with the right people in London. As fervent admirers of the Beatles, they hoped to interest Brian Epstein in managing them. Before leaving Australia, they had sent tapes to his office. But the Bee Gees did not particularly interest Epstein. They did, however, attract the attention of one of his staff, a fellow Australian named Robert Stigwood. Shortly after their arrival in London, the boys got a call from Stigwood's secretary — who was later to become Barry's wife. She asked if the boys were interested in meeting with Stigwood, and Barry replied, "We're interested in meeting with anyone."

Apparently that first meeting between the Bee Gees and their future manager was rather unusual. The brothers swear that Stigwood could hardly stay awake during their audition. But he had already decided to sign the group on the basis of their tapes. "I was absolutely knocked out with their writing," he told *Record World*. "I thought it was sensational. . . . The best new writers to emerge since Lennon and McCartney. . . . The day after they arrived, I had a meeting with them and offered them a deal for recording, management, and publishing."

At that time, Stigwood was not a major power in the music business. His main function was assisting Brian Epstein with the Beatles' affairs. But when Epstein died, Stigwood used his position to form his own company. Since that time, he has become one of the two or three most powerful men in the music industry.

One short month after signing a five-year contract with Stigwood, the Bee Gees released their first international hit — "New York Mining Disaster 1941." When the song was first released, many disc jockeys were mysterious about who the group was. "Here's a new record by an English group whose name begins with a *B*," the jockeys would tease. "See if you can guess who this group is."

Coincidentally, listeners had been waiting for the latest Beatles' release at that time. So for a while, many people actually believed that they were hearing the Beatles. There can be little doubt that Stigwood encouraged this mixup. Barry did sound something like John Lennon on this song, and some of the brothers' harmonies and phrasing resembled the Beatles. But in spite of the similarities, it was clear even on "New York Mining Disaster 1941" that the Bee Gees had their own musical identity.

An important part of the group's sound was the rich orchestral backing that was prominent on most of their work in the sixties. But the Bee Gees also had to make live appearances and wanted to have a lineup similar to other contemporary groups. Throughout their early years, they had worked mostly as a vocal trio with Barry on guitar and Maurice on bass. Now for the first time, the Bee Gees became a quintet, adding Vince Melouney on guitar and Colin Peterson on drums.

With the heavy push of Robert Stigwood's aggressive management, the Bee Gees were on the road to becoming superstars. In May of 1967, they made their British TV debut on *Top of the Pops*. The Bee Gees' appearance on this show was a sure sign that the group had made it in England. Their single was sweeping the nation, and within a few weeks it had made the top twenty in the United States. Not only that, listeners were flipping the record over and checking out the B side — "I Can't See Nobody." This song is actually more typical of the early Bee Gees sound than "New York Mining Disaster 1941." It features Robin's quivering, pleading tenor voice — a trademark of many of the group's romantic ballads.

By the time the *Bee Gees First* LP was released, it was clear that this group was no flash in the pan. While many listeners raved about the great singing, it was the Bee Gees' songwriting that interested other artists. No less than forty-seven singers have recorded "Words," including Elvis Presley. "How Can You Mend a Broken Heart," has been recorded by performers as diverse as Al Green, Johnny Mathis, and Cher. Bee Gees' songs have been sung by rock singers like Janis Joplin, and Eric Burdon; country stars like Roy Orbison, and Brenda Lee, and middle-of-the-road performers like Andy Williams, and the Sandpipers.

As well-respected as their songwriting is, the brothers refuse to overrate the importance of their lyrics. It is well known that they have written some of their most popular songs in a few minutes' time. In an interview with *Rolling Stone*, Robin compared the group's method of knocking off songs to the way most people write postcards. The way he tells it, "New York Mining Disaster 1941" was written in a dark hallway; "I Can't See Nobody" was written in a nightclub dressing room, and "Jive Talking" was composed while driving down a causeway in Miami.

It is not surprising that many rock critics get upset when they learn that songs can be turned out with so little effort. Still, it is hard to fault the lyrics or the music of most Bee Gees songs. The brothers just know how to put together a popular tune, but they have never called their lyrics poetry. "Some of our lyrics have been written just to make people think enough to get from one line to the next," Barry told *Record World*. "And sometimes craziness — pure insanity — can take you there just the same. . . . Most of our stuff I think is great, but we've done some rubbish as well."

By 1968, the Bee Gees were well on their way as both songwriters and recording artists. But there were still some kinks to iron out. The group's sound depended on huge orchestras, complete with violins and cellos. They simply could not duplicate their records with a five-piece rock band.

For a year after their first hit, Stigwood did not let the group appear in England or in the States. When he finally did arrange a concert at London's Royal Albert Hall, the group was accompanied by a sixty-piece orchestra. A few months later, the Bee Gees again used an orchestra at their first American concert at New York's Forest Hills Stadium. Robert Stigwood regards that night as one of the high points of the group's career.

"It was an outdoor concert and it was raining. They did about an hour and a half in the rain, but I don't think one person in the audience moved. I've never seen a reaction at a concert like that. The audience just wouldn't let them off the stage and gave them a thirty-minute ovation at the end. That was their first big New York appearance, and it was really great to see."

The Bee Gees should have been delirious with joy. They had finally made their mark as live performers, and their record sales were increasing with each new release. But all was not well. The brothers were having difficulties with their musical and personal lives. There were a number of ego problems which surfaced on their first American tour. Barry had always been the group's leader, main writer, and most versatile singer. It is not difficult to understand how Robin — who had the most unique voice — could have felt overshadowed by his older brother.

Barry freely admits that most of the conflicts were between him and Robin, with Maurice caught in the middle. In an interview with *Record World*, Barry discussed the problems that led to the group's fifteen-month breakup in 1969. "The first year of success is always great. All brains are working together, and there's no jealousy. But things happen to screw that up — the road, having a second or third hit record, and then all of a sudden having to cope with things you didn't think about before. There comes a point where nothing seems realistic any more."

One of the things that must have seemed especially un-
realistic was the sudden wealth and fame the Bee Gees were
experiencing for the first time. "It was ridiculous," Maurice
said recently. "Before I was twenty-one, I could look down
my street, and every car, from the Rolls Royce in front of
the house to the Aston Martin at the end of the block, belonged to me." Maurice had also developed a fairly heavy
drinking problem and a reputation for smashing up his expensive cars. As a result of these trying experiences, he no
longer drives at all. Looking back at those troubled times,
Maurice confesses, "I was getting to be a real alky." And he
wasn't the only Bee Gee with personal problems. During
that same period, Robin was often spaced-out on pills, and
Barry was also overindulging in drugs.

So the group broke up. Robin was the first to leave, announcing that he was planning to pursue a career as a solo
singer. Barry and Maurice continued to record as the Bee
Gees. But in November 1969, Barry also decided to try his
luck at a solo and film career. The Bee Gees were now officially defunct.

Dick Ashby, who has worked as the Bee Gees' road manager for years, was on tour with them when they split up. As
someone who actually ate and slept with the brothers, he
has one of the best perspectives on the troubles that were
brewing at the time of the breakup. He explained the situation to *Record World* this way:

> Imagine this: the twins were seventeen, Barry was nineteen,
> and within a year of arriving in England they were driving
> around in Rolls Royces and they had as much money as you
> could want. You can see what it did to their heads. . . . Who
> are any of us to condemn that. . . . What would it do to us? I
> don't know what it would have done to me if I had God
> knows how much money, and a Rolls Royce, and a Tudor
> mansion when I was seventeen years old. Obviously, egos
> played a big part in it, and they just got to the point where the

whole thing needed a rest. They needed that break so they could sit back and assess the situation, become more mature and sensible, and then get back together. I think it was something that had to happen. Also, of course, they lived together for (many) years before then. . . . Normal families sometimes get a bit tense. You can imagine what it was like after all those years.

Compared to the music they made as a group, the brothers' solo efforts were nothing to sing about. Of the three, Robin was the most successful by far. His album — *Robin's Reign* — contained several singles that were hits in England. Barry and Maurice also released singles, but neither of them went very far.

When the Bee Gees finally did get back together, it was Robin who made the first move to reunite the group. Although his solo efforts were fairly well received, he wasn't really happy working alone. "When you're doing something on your own and have success, you can't really share it with anyone," he told *Record World*. "I was in my house watching television one day, feeling somewhat (ticked) off 'cause I realized what we were doing, or what we were all trying to do separately, was what we could all do together. Barry was in Spain. . . . I rang him up and said — 'Let's get back together and go into the studio.' He said we'd have to talk about it when he got back to London. Well, it wasn't as easy as that. It was six months later when we finally got around to getting into the studio. . . ."

It took a while for the Bee Gees to get back to where they were before the breakup. Their comeback single — "Lonely Days" — was a big hit. Two successful albums and the huge hit single — "How Can You Mend a Broken Heart" —came out of those same sessions. But in general, their work during the early seventies lacked the spark of the first three albums. The Bee Gees may have been back together, but they were also in a musical rut.

On their next few albums, the group sounded bogged down in their romantic ballad formula. Many critics were calling their sound "gooey and melodramatic." There were a few good moments on *Life in a Tin Can* and *Mr. Natural*. But for the most part, the Bee Gees considered this music out of step with the times. There was still a demand for the group at concerts. The brothers had assembled a new band and were playing to cheering audiences all over the world. But without any current hit records, the Bee Gees were in danger of becoming a nice memory from another time.

"We were just doing ballads back then, because that's what we thought everybody wanted to hear from us," Maurice admits now. In an era dominated by hard rock and finger-snapping R&B, the Bee Gees were moving in a direction that Barry now calls, "wrongheaded." But in 1975, the group got back on the right track. Together with Arif Mardin — a highly regarded R&B producer who had worked with Aretha Franklin — the Bee Gees came up with a new sound. There had always been some black influence in the group's music, although they were not really aware of how to put it to good use. Thanks to Mardin's input on the *Main Course* album, this all changed.

Of the three brothers, Barry always had the strongest interest in black music. He credits Otis Redding as the singer whose phrasing most influenced him. In fact, when he wrote "To Love Somebody," Barry hoped that Otis would someday record the song. Mardin quickly picked up Barry's R&B tendencies and suggested that he try to sing in a high falsetto voice. The experiment worked out so well that it became an important part of the new Bee Gees' sound. The other new wrinkle that Mardin added was a strong R&B dance beat. He encouraged the brothers to write different kinds of songs that would put their strong vocals in a livelier, more commercial setting.

Mardin believes that the Bee Gees were able to alter their musical direction because of a rare flexibility and openness to new ideas. "There are certain artists to whom everything is sacred," he told *Record World*. "They cannot change any notes, you can't touch it. But the Bee Gees aren't like that at all. They're open for suggestions. . . . For example, I might say, 'Why don't we start with the chorus, it's a stronger line.' And they'd say, 'Okay.' "

The sound Mardin and the Bee Gees came up with on songs like "Jive Talking," and "Nights on Broadway," was not just ordinary disco. It was, rather, a combination of strings, synthesizers, horns, and rhythm which was custom-fitted to the group's unique vocals. The Bee Gees had listened carefully to R&B artists — particularly the Impressions, and Stevie Wonder — and come up with their own groove. "We're always collecting ideas for songs by looking around us," Barry told *Hit Parader*. "Everybody's dancing now and people should be able to dance to our music."

Unfortunately, this happy marriage between the Bee Gees and Arif Mardin was to be short-lived. When the group's record label, RSO, terminated its relationship with Atlantic Records in 1976, the Bee Gees were no longer permitted to use Mardin as their producer. But they learned much from him. Their later records, coproduced with Karl Richardson and Albby Gaulten, built on the sound which Mardin helped them perfect. The brothers' first album on RSO — *Children of the World* — contained two hit singles in a similar R&B style: "You Should Be Dancing," and "Love So Right." Along with their change in musical direction, the Bee Gees also recaptured their magic touch. They were, once again, among the top recording acts in the business.

On their first live album — *Here at Last* — Barry, Robin,

The Bee Gees—in the recording studio, laying down a vocal track.
Record World—RSO Records

and Maurice presented an impressive retrospective of their
work from 1967–1976. The two-record set, which features a
good sampling of both early ballads and later up-tempo
numbers, clearly established the brothers among the most
prolific writers and important performers in rock history.
The Bee Gees might well have considered themselves at the
very top of their careers. But in 1977, something happened
that must have made all that went before it seem small. That
something can be summed up in three words — *Saturday
Night Fever.*

The Bee Gees were at the famous Chateau D'Herouville
Studios in France, mixing the *Here at Last* album, when they
got a call from Robert Stigwood. He was in the process of
producing a new movie and wanted the brothers to write a
soundtrack for it. Stigwood believed strongly in the film
and its new young star, John Travolta. All he needed now

was the right music. Apparently, the Bee Gees wrote five of the songs for *Saturday Night Fever* in just one week. One of them — "Staying Alive" — was supposedly written in a mere two hours. The group did not sing every song in the film, although they wrote and produced all the original material, including "Emotion," sung by Samantha Sang and "If I Can't Have You" performed by Yvonne Elliman.

Saturday Night Fever is the best-selling album in music business history — 27-million copies have been sold at this writing. Not only that, the Bee Gees became the first performers to have six straight number-one singles, and five records in the top ten at the same time. Three of these songs — "Stayin Alive," "Night Fever," and "How Deep Is Your Love" — were written and sung by the group. The other two — Samantha Sang's "Emotion," and younger brother Andy Gibb's "Love Is Thicker Than Water" —were written and produced by the Bee Gees.

The enormous success of *Saturday Night Fever* has made the Bee Gees a dominating force in popular music. Because of their writing and producing talents, the brothers' influence has been particularly strong. An interesting difference between the Bee Gees and other superstars is that the brothers have come this far without a particularly strong personal appeal. Elvis Presley had his sneering grin and swiveling hips. The Beatles came across with originality and wit. Both had qualities that went beyond their music; personalities that affected the lifestyles of their audiences. But the Bee Gees do not have this kind of charisma. They have reached the top only because their music is so appealing.

This is not to say that the Bee Gees don't excite live audiences — they do. Barry is even appealing enough to be considered a heart-throb. Mainly though, the brothers just walk up on stage and give the audience a tight set chock-full of hit songs. There is nothing particularly unique or exciting about the way they perform; no profound social messages in their songs, and nothing especially original about the way they see the world.

Nevertheless, the Brothers Gibb are superstars. And like all superstars, they pay a price for their fame and fortune. They are all multimillionaires, having earned an estimated fifteen million dollars in 1977 alone. A few years ago, they moved their base of operations from England to Florida's luxurious Biscayne Bay. They are also all happily married, with children. Much has been made of the close family feeling among the Gibbs, and it definitely is a most unusual thing to behold among rock stars. The Gibbs — including Mom, Dad, and singing brother Andy — all live close together. Unlike most superstars, there are no groupies in the dressing room after the shows and very little gossip in the fan magazines.

Still, privacy is a big problem for the Bee Gees. Tour boats haunt the shores of Barry's waterfront mansion, as fans call out and snap their cameras. Bus loads of curious tourists come up to the front gate by the hour, hoping to get a glimpse of their favorite Bee Gee. This kind of constant disruption makes it difficult to lead a normal life. As great as it is to be a superstar with untold riches, it can get downright depressing to feel trapped in your own house. "Sometimes," Barry complains, "it feels like you're living in a bloody goldfish bowl."

The Bee Gees also want to be sure not to get trapped in the wrong musical direction. Barry has recently indicated that he is getting tired of disco and might want to make some different kinds of records. He also wants to get away from a vocal sound built mostly around his high-pitched falsetto — a sound that one critic compared to the "shrieking of electric mice." Instead, the brothers would like to compose more songs for Robin's vulnerable tenor and Barry's dynamic middle-range voice.

Spirits Having Flown, the Bee Gees' follow-up to *Saturday*

Night Fever, saw a return to a more lush and syrupy sound. The first single off the album, "Too Much Heaven," was closer to middle-of-the-road than to rock or R&B. And "Tragedy," the second release, was an odd combination of sentimental lyrics with a disco beat. Both songs featured Barry's falsetto, and neither could compare to "Staying Alive," or "How Deep Is Your Love." Still, the album and both singles were number-one hits. With *Spirits Having Flown*, the Bee Gees seem to be moving toward a more conventional pop sound and away from the R&B flavors of "Jive Talking," and "Night Fever."

But the Brothers Gibb are not concerned with musical labels like rock, pop, disco, R&B, etc. To them, it's all just the business of making popular music. They rarely refer to their work as art. Rather, they speak of creating music to please people. Many rock critics have trouble with the Bee Gees' approach. They believe that a true rock *artist* should be concerned with matters other than merely turning out commercial product. But the Bee Gees make no such pretenses. They don't consider themselves rock artists, rhythm and blues artists, or any other kind of artists. They are simply talented and skilled craftsmen who know how to make good popular music in many different styles.

Barry, Robin, and Maurice are presently in as good a position as anyone to influence the course of popular music in the 1980's. Aside from their collective efforts, the brothers all plan to be doing projects on their own. Barry — who has already written and produced a series of hits for kid-brother Andy — will be trying to do the same for Barbra Streisand. Robin is working with two highly respected R&B artists — Tina Turner and David Ruffin. Maurice has also had offers to produce, but thinks he may study acting at London's Royal Academy of Dramatic Art instead.

As a matter of fact, all of the brothers have expressed a

desire to act at one time or another. But aside from their disappointing appearance in *Sgt. Pepper's Lonely Heart's Club Band*, none of them have yet found the time to pursue these ambitions. The *Sgt. Pepper* movie was almost all music, and the Bee Gees did no real acting. Although their desire to act was probably the motivation for accepting the film, this project never should have been undertaken. A group as well established as the Bee Gees can only hurt its own credibility by dressing up in silly costumes and singing third-rate versions of Beatles tunes. Before *Sgt. Pepper*, the brothers never had recorded a song they didn't write. To a man, the Bee Gees admit that the project was a fiasco. They must know that someday soon there is bound to be a sound-alike, look-alike group being hyped as follows:

BEE GEE MANIA — It's not the Bee Gees, but an incredible simulation. If you didn't see the Bee Gees in the 1970's, this is about as close as you're going to get.

Yes, the possibility of Bee Gees nostalgia in the 1980's is not at all farfetched. After a triumphant thirteen-week, thirty-eight-city tour that culminated in a ninety-minute TV special in November, 1979, the group was talking about splitting up again.

"With this tour, all the hyperactivity began to take its toll," Barry told *Us* magazine. "I found myself either on top of the world or totally depressed. A couple of times I was at the point of bursting into tears. Being Bee Gees is like three people being one person. It's impossible. We are each of us having an identity crisis. It could drive us all crazy."

It is easy to understand why the brothers might want to split for a while. As much as they deny it, Barry is recognized as the major talent in the group. Robin, in particular, may want a chance to emerge from out of his older brother's shadow. There are also the many pressures that success brings. The constant crush of spending weeks in the studio and then going on tour for months to support each album can take its toll. This kind of lifestyle has been known to wear people down in a hurry. But the Bee Gees know the pitfalls. After all, they've been down this road before.

BEE GEES COLLECTORS' GUIDE
— Smash Hit

ALBUMS

Year	Album	Label	Hit
1967	Bee Gees' First	Atco	*
1968	Horizontal	Atco	*
1968	Idea	Atco	*
1968	Rare Precious and Beautiful Volume 1	Atco	
1969	Odessa	Atco	*
1969	Best of Bee Gees	Atco	*
1970	Rare Precious and Beautiful Volume 2	Atco	
1970	Robin's Reign	Atco	
1970	Cucumber Castle	Atco	
1971	Two Years On	Atco	
1971	Trafalgar	Atco	
1972	To Whom It May Concern	Atco	
1973	Life in a Tin Can	RSO	
1973	Best of Bee Gees—Volume 2	RSO	
1974	Mr. Natural	RSO	
1975	Main Course	RSO	*
1976	Children of the World	RSO	*

ALBUMS

Year	Album	Label	Hit
1976	*Bee Gees Gold, Volume 1*	RSO	*
1976	*Odessa*	RSO	
1977	*Here at Last . . . Bee Gees . . . Live*	RSO	*
1977	*Saturday Night Fever*	RSO	*
1979	*Spirits Having Flown*	RSO	*
1979	*Bee Gees' Greatest*	RSO	*

SINGLES

Year	Single	Label	Hit
1967	*New York Mining Disaster 1941*	Atco	*
1967	*To Love Somebody*	Atco	*
1967	*Holiday*	Atco	*
1967	*Massachusetts*	Atco	*
1967	*Words*	Atco	*
1968	*Singer Sang His Song/Jumbo*	Atco	
1968	*I've Got to Get a Message to You*	Atco	*
1968	*I Started a Joke*	Atco	*
1969	*The First of May*	Atco	
1969	*Tomorrow Tomorrow*	Atco	
1969	*Don't Forget to Remember*	Atco	
1970	*If Only I Had My Mind on Something Else/ L.O.I.O.*	Atco	
1971	*Lonely Days*	Atco	*
1971	*How Can You Mend a Broken Heart*	Atco	*
1971	*Don't Wanna Live Inside Myself*	Atco	
1972	*My World*	Atco	*
1972	*Run to Me*	Atco	*
1972	*Alive*	Atco	
1973	*Saw a New Morning*	RSO	
1974	*Mr. Natural*	RSO	
1975	*Jive Talking*	RSO	*

SINGLES

Year	Single	Label	Hit
1975	*Nights on Broadway*	RSO	*
1975	*Fanny (Be Tender with My Love)*	RSO	
1976	*You Should Be Dancing*	RSO	*
1976	*Love So Right*	RSO	*
1977	*Boogie Child*	RSO	*
1977	*Edge of the Universe*	RSO	
1977	*How Deep Is Your Love*	RSO	*
1977	*Stayin' Alive*	RSO	*
1978	*Night Fever*	RSO	*
1979	*Too Much Heaven*	RSO	*
1979	*Tragedy*	RSO	*
1979	*Love You Inside Out*	RSO	*

Guitar Giants

5. ERIC CLAPTON

A NUMBER OF rock's greatest heroes have been magical guitar players. One of the first was Chuck Berry, the creator of the legendary "Johnny B. Goode." This young country picker could, "play a guitar just like ringin' a bell," and people would come from miles around just to hear him. "Johnny B." had a gift for fast and flashy guitar playing, and so did Eric Clapton.

Like most rock guitarists, Eric learned to play by imitating the classic rhythms and licks of Chuck Berry. By the time he joined the Yardbirds at age eighteen, he had mastered this style. There were other important guitar players moving in the same direction — Keith Richards, Brian Jones, and Jeff Beck to name a few. But to the London rock crowd, E.C. was number one. *"Clapton is God."* They screamed it from the audience; they even wrote it on the walls of subway stations.

115

Unlike most of the fans, Eric was not impressed with the speed and flash of his guitar work. His musical abilities came without much effort. But Eric understood that the creation of truly meaningful music was no easy task. There would have to be much soul searching and dues paying before he could truly express himself. He found his inspiration in the work of authentic country bluesmen like Robert Johnson, Big Bill Broonzy, and Skip James. Clapton also adapted the styles of contemporary blues guitarists such as B.B. and Albert King.

"I just got completely overwhelmed with the blues," Eric told a writer for *Rolling Stone*. "I studied it and listened to it and went right down in it and came back up in it." The Yardbirds provided Eric an outlet for playing the blues. They even made an album with an authentic Mississippi bluesman — *Sonny Boy Williamson and the Yardbirds*. But

Eric Clapton—rock 'n' roll survivor
Record World—RSO Records

after a year and a half, E.C. became disenchanted with the group. Originally, he was attracted to the life of a pop star. But as he immersed himself in the blues, E.C.'s values began to change. "I started to take music as a serious thing," he told *Rolling Stone*. "I just realized I'd be doing it for the rest of my life and I'd better be doing it right."

After Eric left the Yardbirds in 1964, he felt depressed enough to consider giving up the guitar altogether. One thing for certain, E.C. had no intention of joining another pop group. But when John Mayall offered him a job, Eric accepted. Mayall was recognized as Britain's foremost blues purist. His band played straight-ahead Chicago blues. Unlike the Yardbirds, Mayall had no interest in trying to make hit records.

E.C.'s playing on Mayall's *Bluesbreakers* album made him a major figure in the 1960's blues revival. Rock fans both in England and in the United States were developing a growing interest in the blues. For the first time, authentic blues musicians like Muddy Waters, and B.B. King were working regularly at concerts and clubs with predominately young white audiences. As much as the rock crowd responded to the great black bluesmen, they were far more turned on by the faster and more dazzling playing of Clapton. The black fathers had the substance, but the young white boys — like Eric, and Mike Bloomfield — had the flash.

Until Jimi Hendrix came along and blew everybody else out of the ballpark, E.C. was the most dazzling guitar player of his generation. Still, he cared little about the flashiness which came so naturally. For Eric, electric blues guitar playing was a simple music to master. So simple, he often wondered if his great speed and dazzling runs were nothing more than slick tricks.

There was something deeper in the blues for Eric. Something that went beyond questions of technique. It wasn't just a matter of playing your instrument. Authentic blues artists lived the lives they sang about. And it was all there in the music — the pain, the humor, and the struggle to survive. By studying the blues and the men who lived them, Eric hoped to evolve his own original and personal music.

Of all the great blues artists who influenced Eric's development, the legendary Robert Johnson was the most important. Although he was a self-accompanied Mississippi picker who recorded in the 1930's, Johnson has been called the first rock 'n' roller. It wasn't only that he pioneered many of the lines and rhythms that laid the foundation for modern electric blues playing. Robert Johnson's music actually captured the spirit of rock 'n' roll.

Aside from the twenty-six sides he recorded in a makeshift studio in a Dallas hotel room, there are few facts known about Johnson's life. Son House, another great Mississippi blues picker, remembers a time when Johnson could hardly play the guitar. At one point, House recalls, Johnson disappeared for about a year. When he returned, he was an awesome musician who had developed his art far beyond his contemporaries. Most religious, self-respecting black folks considered the blues a sinful music, and blues musicians, in league with Satan. But when Son House and the other backwoods pickers heard Robert Johnson's music, even they believed that the only way a man could play like that was by selling his soul to the devil.

Nobody knows for sure how Johnson acquired his musical prowess. But the small body of work that is his legacy clearly establishes him as the most important blues musician America has ever produced. The music he made with his voice and guitar, accompanied only by his stomping feet, sounds like a complete band. Indeed, the next generation of blues singers simply hired three or four sidemen to play the lines that Johnson was doing by himself.

Clapton was more than impressed with how much music

Johnson could create on his own. To reproduce this feat in an electric setting, he had to go beyond the conventional Chicago blues format Mayall's band provided. E.C. wanted to explore other musical and emotional possibilities. There was a sense of struggle in the music of Robert Johnson which struck a chord deep in E.C.'s soul. Johnson's struggle concerned the evil and deceitful women in his life — one of whom eventually murdered him. But Johnson's problems went beyond women, and even beyond the violence that wandering black musicians often encountered in the South. He was a man fighting against dark and unknown forces within himself.

Writer Greil Marcus summed up the questions Robert Johnson asked in his music as follows: "What is man's place in the world? Why is he cursed with the power to want more than he can have? What separates men and women from each other? Why must they suffer guilt, not only for their sins, but for the failure of their best hopes?"

It was Eric Clapton's deepest wish to reach a point that his music would address itself to these issues. He certainly was wrestling with them personally for years. But E.C. had a long way to go before he understood the best way to use his brilliant guitar skills. Also, his singing and songwriting talents were relatively undeveloped, and he sorely wanted to progress in these areas. Still, Eric knew that he was a "heavy" guitar player. For the time being anyway, that would have to do.

Together with bassist Jack Bruce and drummer Ginger Baker, Clapton formed Cream. The band was the power trio that became the prototype for hundreds of other "heavy metal" groups which formed in that mold. The idea of Cream was for three great musicians to play as forcefully as possible. This meant that the drums and bass functioned as lead instruments instead of assuming their usual backup roles. During his time with the group, Clapton was quick to point out the differences between Cream and bands like the Jimi Hendrix Experience. "The Experience is built around Jimi's guitar playing," Eric once told this writer. "But Cream has no lead instrument. We're all three equally important."

The fact is that the members of Cream reckoned they were the best rock players around. Thus the name Cream, as in *cream* of the crop. Like E.C., Bruce and Baker had mastered the blues, rhythm and blues, and pop-rock styles, and were ready to take them to places unknown. "We aimed to start a revolution in musical thought," Eric reflects. "We set out to change the world, to upset people and to shock them."

They also pleased and excited millions of people. For a group that disregarded all the conventions of turning out three-minute hits, they were amazingly popular. Cream redefined rock as music in which the players were free to take long, improvised solos. Both Eric, and Jack Bruce collaborated with lyricist Pete Brown in writing most of Cream's original material. Brown's lyrics were quite unusual compared to most ordinary pop songs. And many of the melodies contributed by Clapton and Bruce were equally uncommon.

The group's albums did well, mixing originals with blues material. There was even a number-one single — "The Sunshine of Your Love." But to really appreciate Cream, you needed to see them live. Their approach to music owed much to jazz improvisation. Never before had a group of superstars played with such abandon. As one noted jazz musician remarked at the time: "These dudes were definitely stretching out." One of the highlights of any Cream concert was Ginger Baker's twenty-minute solo in "Toad." *That's* what the fans came to hear. The Cream were heavy musicians, and audiences filled the halls to hear them play. To hear Clapton, Bruce, and Baker "get it on."

Unquestionably, Cream was the first rock group to have such an impact primarily on the strength of its instrumental work. Most major rock groups based their success on good songwriting and distinctive vocals. But looking back, it is clear that Cream did cause a revolution in rock. Writer Lloyd Grossman in his book — *A Social History of Rock Music* — summed up the impact of Cream this way:

> More than any other rock group of the time, more than the Beatles or the Stones or The Who, Cream broke with the tradition of pop music. Their first album, *Fresh Cream*, was a bombshell, a red flag that signaled that there could never — that there should never — be a return to the safe and acceptable (harmless kind of) bland three-minute pop tunes with pretty melodies.
>
> That was the promise of Cream in 1966; a promise of liberation — not from commercialism, because after all Cream made far more money than most rock groups, but from the constriction and the monotony of the three-minute pop song. . . . (They offered) a promise of a new pop music era in which free, unrestrained, savage music-making would be financially (profitable) to the music industry, and (artistically) acceptable to the audience. This promise like all good promises went unfulfilled.

By the summer of 1968 the group confirmed the widespread rumors of its breakup. They announced a fall tour of major arenas that would be their last. Perhaps it should have been obvious from the beginning that Cream would burn itself out in a relatively short time. The official reason for the breakup had something to do with having gone as far musically as they possibly could. But the truth is that there were a number of serious musical differences among the members. To some extent, the problems appear to have gotten personal. At least once during the final tour, Jack

Bruce pointed to Ginger Baker after a long drum solo and said: "Ginger Baker folks. The *great* Ginger Baker." Not to be outdone, Baker pointed and shouted: "Let's hear it for Jack Bruce-Eric Clapton, ladies and gentlemen." The tone in Ginger's voice was not one of humor and good fellowship.

This incident points out Cream's difficulties as well as anything. The group has often been described as three perfect jewels that could shine but not fuse. Ultimately, most quality bands depend on teamwork to survive. Like a great basketball team, there have to be some people willing to pass the ball and let others take the limelight, but because Cream was conceived as *three heavy musicians* doing their thing simultaneously, there wasn't too much concern about cooperation.

A few months before the group's breakup, Eric heard some tapes which profoundly changed his attitude about Cream's music. These tapes were to later surface as albums — *Music from Big Pink* by The Band (1969) and *The Basement Tapes* by Bob Dylan and The Band (officially released in 1974, although bootleg versions had been available since 1968). The Band also consisted of very accomplished musicians, but their approach to music was the exact opposite of Cream's. Instead of playing with abandon, The Band exercised control and restraint. The idea was for each member to find a role in the music that enhanced what the others were doing. Robbie Robertson — The Band's main writer, and a guitarist at least as important as Clapton, choose to de-emphasize his own role. Instead of taking long and loud solos, Robertson choose to allow the vocals to interweave with the textures created by The Band as a whole. When he did take a solo, it was so effective and so restrained that the work of most other rock guitarists sounded excessive and long-winded by comparison.

"When I heard The Band," Eric has often said, "I knew

that it was all over for Cream." What he heard was a music that came closer to the spirit of what he envisioned for himself. Hearing the all-for-one approach of The Band had made Cream's efforts seem somewhat superficial and self-centered.

Eric was also impressed with the way Robertson and Dylan wrote songs. Their work had depth and substance, but still retained a melodic quality that was missing in most of Cream's writing. The music of Dylan and The Band was original, yet it drew strength from the traditions of blues, gospel, and country music. Eric decided that his next band would be modeled along these lines. He never again wanted to be in a group that emphasized the dazzling technique of its players.

But just before Cream disbanded, Eric gave one of his most memorable performances with the group — a live version of Robert Johnson's "Crossroads." E.C.'s tribute to his mentor was the highlight of the *Wheels of Fire* album. Thirty years after Johnson sang about being stranded after dark in a racist Southern town, E.C. was able to give the

Cream—forerunner of a thousand heavy-metal groups: Eric Clapton (left), Ginger Baker, and Jack Bruce.
Record World—Atlantic Records

words a new vitality. And Johnson's musical vision took on a new brillance when reinterpreted by the three-piece electric band.

"Crossroads Blues" By Robert Johnson

I went down to the crossroads, fell down on my knees.
I went down to the crossroads, fell down on my knees.
Ask the Lord above for mercy, say boy if you please.

Standing at the crossroads, I tried to flag a ride.
Standing at the crossroads, I tried to flag a ride.
But nobody seem to know me, everybody passed me by. . . .

Yeah I'm standing at the crossroads, I believe I'm sinking down.

After the breakup of Cream, E.C. did not stand at the crossroads for long. A few short months later, he had formed a new band, Blind Faith. On the surface, the combination of Clapton and English singer, keyboard player, guitarist Stevie Winwood seemed like a natural. Winwood, who wrote, sang, and played organ on the 1963 hit "Gimme Some Loving," was recognized as England's greatest rock singer. He was also an exceptional organist, as well as a creative guitar player. Winwood's work with the group, Traffic, in the late sixties had some great moments, but it was generally recognized that the other musicians in the group weren't up to his level. The thought of E.C. and Winwood in the same band sparked the imagination of rock fans.

Unfortunately, Blind Faith meant only one thing to the moguls of the music industry — another supergroup and more big bucks. Surprisingly, Ginger Baker was asked to play drums. This made it seem that Jack Bruce had been the culprit in Cream's personal hassles. In any case, Blind

Faith's bassist, Rick Grech, was probably picked because he *wasn't* well known. So what we had here was still another supergroup — three superstars and a sideman. Even the name Blind Faith implied that the music just had to be great! Look at the heavies that were making it!

Not surprisingly, the band was doomed before it ever really got rolling. Eric admitted afterwards that he was unhappy with the group's lineup: "Ginger and Rick were never part of my plans," he recalls. All the high hopes for the Clapton-Winwood alliance also didn't work out. E.C. has always been shy about his singing. He freely admits that he is an ordinary singer who needed encouragement to step in front of a microphone. In his earlier groups, Eric was content to leave the singing to others who were either better or more assertive. Still, he always made some vocal contributions. But Stevie Winwood was so great that E.C. felt even more inadequate about his own voice. Thus, he did no singing at all with Blind Faith.

Stevie Winwood recalls that he knew the group was a hype as soon as it was called Blind Faith. And when music-business heavy Robert Stigwood started booking the band in huge arenas like New York's Madison Square Garden, that was really the beginning of the end. It was just another case of a musical situation being taken over by businessmen. So what if the band hadn't really gotten themselves together musically? When there are millions of dollars to be made, someone is going to try and cash in.

E.C. was disgusted after Blind Faith's (people had begun to call the group No Faith) first tour. As far as he was concerned, that phase of his career was over. He had developed a close friendship with the opening act on the Blind Faith tour — Delaney and Bonnie & Friends — and was sitting in with them regularly. Delaney and Bonnie's music was a combination of southern rock, country, and

R&B — just the kind of stuff Eric longed to play. Together with Delaney and several of the band's sidemen, Eric recorded his first solo album — *Eric Clapton.* This was the first LP that featured Eric as the main singer and writer.

E.C. was so comfortable playing with Delaney and his friends that he convinced several of the musicians to come to England and join his new band — *Derek and the Dominoes.* Together with bassist Carl Radle, drummer Jim Gordon, and keyboard man Bobby Whitlock, Eric was to achieve the high point of his musical career. He was also about to experience the toughest three years of his life.

Eric's search had always involved more than music. There was a deep feeling of loneliness and emptiness that had haunted him for years. During the Blind Faith tour, Eric became deeply interested in Christianity. One of the highlights of the *Blind Faith* album was Clapton's composition, "In the Presence of the Lord." But by the time Derek and the Dominoes recorded their only studio album, Eric had other emotional problems. He had been pursuing a love affair with the wife of his close friend — Beatle George Harrison. When Patti Harrison decided to return to her husband, Eric hit rock bottom. In his despair, he turned from religion to drugs.

On the *Layla* album, Eric finally combined his musical and personal experiences to create his most moving work. There were a number of good songs on the album including Jimi Hendrix's "Little Wing," and the great blues classic "Have You Ever Loved a Woman." But the high point of the album was the song "Layla," an anthem to Eric's lost love. In this one song, E.C. finally succeeded in adapting the blues into his own personal statement. At last, he had reached the raw emotion of Robert Johnson without copying him. Indeed, "Layla" wasn't true blues in terms of musical structure. But it captured the essence of the blues experience more than most standard blues songs ever could. Writer Dave Marsh is correct in noting that among white musicians, only Van Morrison has consistently expressed the blues feeling without relying on blues forms. "For that reason alone," Marsh maintains, " 'Layla's' greatness and its importance to rock history and Clapton's career would be unquestioned."

In the final verse of "Layla," E.C. invokes the words of one of Robert Johnson's great songs, "Love in Vain."

"Please don't say, we'll never find a way.
Or tell me all my love's in vain."

The song then concludes with a beautiful piano solo, embellished with the distinctive slide guitar work of the late Duane Allman. On this magnificent note, Eric withdrew from the public eye and ear for the next three years.

Like a number of his colleagues, Eric Clapton got hooked on heroin. It wasn't going to be easy to kick the habit. But on the other hand, the price of addiction was high. Many rock stars were already dead from constantly abusing drugs. The death of Jimi Hendrix had a particularly profound effect on Eric who confessed, "I was mad at him for not taking me with him." But on the other hand, Eric was not quite ready to commit suicide. Being a junkie was his way of teasing death. Like many people approaching thirty, Eric knew it was time to decide if he wanted to be around for the long haul. The fact that he withdrew from the public life of a rock performer was a strong indication that he would make it. He freely admits that the pressures of the music business were doing as much to destroy him as the poisonous powder he was shooting into his veins.

By the end of 1972, Eric was committed to kicking the habit. He even felt strong enough to allow Pete Townshend of The Who to arrange a concert for him at London's Rainbow Theater. The concert, which also featured Stevie Winwood and Ron Wood, was taped and later released on an album — *Eric Clapton's Rainbow Concert.*

During the next few months, Eric succeeded in kicking heroin with the help of acupuncture. While he was in treatment, he passed the time helping with the chores at a friend's farm in Wales. Then one day in the winter of 1974, E.C. walked into Robert Stigwood's office and announced that he was ready to record an album.

Naturally, Eric wondered if the fans would still buy his records and cheer his performances. But Stigwood was confident that E.C. had not lost his standing as one of rock's hottest attractions. After all, the *Rainbow Theater* album made the top twenty in spite of Eric's long absence. A new studio album backed by some solid touring might put him back on top of the heap.

And so it happened. Eric's *461 Ocean Boulevard* made it to number one on the charts. There was even a hit single from the album — reggae king Bob Marley's song, "I Shot the Sheriff." Critics wondered if this meant that Clapton was "going reggae." He wasn't. In fact, it was hard to pinpoint just which musical direction he was going to take. The album *461 Ocean Boulevard* had evolved with various friends dropping by to join Eric in the studio. These included former Domino Carl Radle, and singer Yvonne Elliman of *Jesus Christ Superstar.*

Clapton had always been partial to the studio jam. He has appeared on many albums over the years, although he isn't always listed on the credits. The most famous of these is the Beatles' *White Album*, which features his powerful solo on "While My Guitar Gently Weeps." So this approach of letting friends drop by to jam and seeing what develops was nothing new.

In recent years, E.C. has continued to use the studio jam with good results. On his *No Reason to Cry* album, recorded in 1976, Eric was joined by Dylan and several members of The Band. One Dylan composition, "Sign Language," features Eric singing a duet with Dylan. It is almost impossible to tell where one voice ends and the other begins. Similarly, when Robbie Robertson joins E.C. for a guitar duet, it sounds like they are both playing tribute to each other. The following year, Eric appeared at The Band's monumental Last Waltz Concert and sang a rousing version of Bobby Bland's "Further On Up the Road." The song featured a crisp interchange of solos between Clapton and Robertson. This time, however, the differences between Robbie's biting attack and Clapton's fluid approach were crystal clear. Both guitarists had started with the traditional blues and evolved their own distinctive styles.

Eric has never stopped seeking new ways to express his originality. He is still trying to be a creative musical force, but the desperation of his earlier years has all but disappeared. He is less interested than he ever was in being recognized as the king of the lead guitar players. "Quite honestly," he recently commented in *Creem* magazine, "I don't think I could play one of those solos on every track. My lead guitar playing has slipped because I'm controlling the band, writing songs, and doing everything else. Consequently, something has to suffer, and the lead guitar playing has probably suffered most of all. I don't listen to clever lead guitar players any more. I'm more interested in total songs."

When a new Eric Clapton record comes out, people have no idea what to expect. His musical vocabulary now includes pretty ballads like "Wonderful Tonite," and bouncy country tunes like, "Lay Down Sally." His approach to things is less intense, more laid back, than it used to be.

"What I'm trying to do is find another way of making music that's distinctly me," Eric told *Creem*. "And if it has to be softer and even unrecognizable at first then that's alright, even if it's not the current trend."

Today, Eric Clapton lives the life of a man at peace with himself. He spends a good deal of time at his country estate in a part of England called Hurtwood Edge. Apparently the restless, haunted days of pursuing Robert Johnson's ghost are now behind him. In a storybook ending which does not fit a blues musician, Eric has even managed to retrieve his lost love. Patti Boyd-Harrison, the heroine of "Layla," came back to him. During the summer of 1979, the two were married at a giant wedding party attended by many of rock's biggest stars, including George Harrison.

Now what would Robert Johnson have said about that?

ERIC CLAPTON COLLECTORS' GUIDE
* — *Smash Hit*

ALBUMS

With the Yardbirds

Year	Album	Label	Hit
1964	*Sonny Boy Williamson and the Yardbirds*	Mercury	
1965	*Yardbirds-For Your Love*	Epic	
1965	*Having a Rave Up with the Yardbirds*	Epic	
1970	*The Yardbirds Featuring Performances by Jeff Beck, Eric Clapton, Jimmy Page*	Epic	

With John Mayall

Year	Album	Label	Hit
1967	*Bluesbreakers*	London	

Cream

Year	Album	Label	Hit
1967	Fresh Cream	Atco	
1967	Disraeli Gears	Atco	*
1968	Wheels of Fire	Atco	*
1969	Goodbye	Atco	*
1969	Best of Cream	Atco	*
1970	Live Cream	Atco	*
1972	Live—Volume II	Atco	
1972	Heavy Cream	Polydor	

Blind Faith

Year	Album	Label	Hit
1969	Blind Faith	Atlantic	*

Solo Career

Year	Album	Label	Hit
1970	Layla (w/Derek and the Dominoes)	Atco	*
1970	On Tour w/Eric Clapton (w/Delaney and Bonnie & Friends)	Atco	
1970	Eric Clapton	Atco	*
1972	History of Eric Clapton	Atco	*
1972	Eric Clapton at His Best	Polydor	
1973	Derek and the Dominoes in Concert	RSO	*
1973	Clapton	Polydor	
1973	Eric Clapton's Rainbow Concert	RSO	*
1974	461 Ocean Boulevard	RSO	*
1975	There's One in Every Crowd	RSO	
1975	E.C. Was Here	RSO	*
1976	No Reason to Cry	RSO	*
1977	Slow Hand	RSO	*
1978	Backless	RSO	*
1980	Just One Night	RSO	*

SINGLES

Cream

Year	Single	Label	Hit
1968	*Sunshine of Your Love*	Atco	*
1968	*Anyone for Tennis*	Atco	
1968	*White Room*	Atco	*
1969	*Crossroads*	Atco	
1969	*Badge*	Atco	

Solo Career

Year	Single	Label	Hit
1970	*Layla*	Atco	*
1970	*After Midnight*	Atco	*
1972	*Let It Rain*	Polydor	
1973	*Bell Bottom Blues*	Polydor	*
1974	*I Shot the Sheriff*	RSO	*
1974	*Willie and the Hind Jive*	RSO	
1975	*Swing Low Sweet Chariot*	RSO	
1975	*Knockin' on Heaven's Door*	RSO	
1976	*Hello Old Friend*	RSO	
1977	*Carnival*	RSO	
1977	*Lay Down Sally*	RSO	*
1978	*Wonderful Tonight*	RSO	
1978	*Promises*	RSO	
1979	*Watch Out for Lucy*	RSO	
1979	*Cocaine/Tulsa Time*	RSO	

Dylan's less-than-spectacular voice, Jimi felt encouraged. He soon got his own group together and called it Jimmy James and the Blue Flames. The band worked small Greenwich Village clubs for very little money. But the word was starting to spread. Jimi Hendrix was beginning to get recognition. ▪

Michael Bloomfield, one of the top guitarists at the time, was working the Cafe Au Go Go, Greenwich Village's best club. A friend advised him to go "check out" the guitar player over at the nearby Cafe Wha. Bloomfield described what happened, in *Guitar Player* magazine:

> I was performing with Paul Butterfield, and I was the hotshot guitarist on the block — I thought I was *it*. . . . I went right across the street and saw him. Hendrix knew who I was, and that day, in front of my eyes, he burned me to death. I didn't even get my guitar out. H-bombs were going off, guided missiles were flying — I can't tell you the sounds he was getting out of his instrument. He was getting every sound I was ever to hear him get in that room with a Stratocaster (guitar), a Twin (small amp), a Maestro fuzz tone, and that was all — he was doing it mainly through extreme volume. How he did this, I wish I understood. He just got right up in my face with that axe (instrument), and I didn't even want to pick up a guitar for the next year.

A few weeks later, Jimi's life took a dramatic turn. Chas Chandler, former bass player for the rock group The Animals, asked him to move to England. Chandler had set up a management company with Englishman Michael Jeffrey and felt that Jimi would become an instant idol with the British rock audience. After several weeks of auditions, Hendrix selected drummer Mitch Mitchell and bass-guitarist Noel Redding to form a new group — the Jimi Hendrix Experience. The trio frizzed their hair and bought a large wardrobe of outrageous clothes. Chandler and Jeffrey wanted to play up Jimi's "freakiness."

Within a short time, the group had a number of hits on the British charts, including: "Hey Joe," "The Wind Cries Mary," and "Fifty-first Anniversary." The English, with a broader acceptance of black artists, loved Jimi. There were a number of fine British guitarists at the time, people like Eric Clapton, Peter Townshend, and Jeff Beck. But even these excellent musicians were awed by Hendrix's almost super-human playing.

After a triumphant European tour, the group was ready to conquer America. The Monkees, who had heard Jimi in Europe, invited the group to be their opening act during an upcoming American tour. But Jimi's erotic gestures and lyrics offended many Monkees' fans and their parents. He was eventually dropped from the tour. This was fine with the group's management, who wanted to play up Jimi's wilder side. The stage was now set for the upcoming Monterey Festival in July, 1967.

Jimi's performance at Monterey launched his career in America. The Experience followed The Who on stage. Peter Townshend, guitarist and leader of The Who, violently smashed his guitar at the end of the group's set. But Jimi went the great English guitarist one better. After a sizzling set, Jimi began playing "Wild Thing." At its conclusion, Jimi poured lighter fluid over his guitar and put a match to it. Afterwards, he received a long, standing ovation and much media attention. Jimi Hendrix was on his way to becoming a star in America.

Several weeks later, the Experience arrived in New York. With the help of several members of the Rascals — a very popular New York-based group with a long string of hits — a number of key bookings were arranged. The first of these was at The Scene, an important music business showcase at that time.

The entire audience at The Scene consisted of musicians and music business executives. Everybody gazed in amazement at the wall of amplifiers and sound equipment on the stage. Hendrix walked out on the stage with his loud clothing, frizzed-up hair, and Indian feathers, followed by Mitchell and Redding. It was immediately clear that the record we had been listening to was no fluke. These three musicians were able to produce the same dense and complex music in live performance.

But there was more to Jimi Hendrix's performance than the music. He was like a mass of energy with no limits. The more amazing things he did on the guitar, the more he wanted to do. His physical contortions, like playing with his teeth and behind his back, seemed as much an expression of frustration as they were performing gimmicks. At some point during the set, Hendrix broke a guitar string. A member of the sound crew came on stage and changed the string while Hendrix continued playing his solo, never missing a beat.

The audience at The Scene was stunned at what they were seeing and hearing. They responded with several standing ovations, and the group obliged the cheering crowd with a two-and-one-half-hour set. When the evening ended, a lot of musicians were wondering if they would have the nerve to ever pick up their instruments again. And one well-known record executive was heard asking another: "Where was this kid, how did we let him slip away?"

The following night, the Experience opened for the Rascals at Central Park. Most of the crowd had never heard of Jimi Hendrix. The show was running late and some of the kids started chanting: "We want the Rascals; we want the Rascals." Jimi came up to the microphone and calmly said: "Hey, give us a chance; we can play too."

The Experience did much more than just play that night. Jimi pulled out all the stops. He put on a show that had most of the amazed crowd on its feet. After playing his usual last song, "Wild Thing," he proceeded to smash his guitar to pieces. After all of this, there were still a few kids shouting for the Rascals, but as the young crowd filed out that night, most of the talk was about Jimi Hendrix.

By this time, the group's first American album, *Are You Experienced*, was released on the Reprise label. The band had received a good deal of publicity, and attracted a sizable following. Still, the Experience was unable to command the status of a top-billed act in major clubs. When Hendrix finally made it to the stage of the Cafe Au Go Go, it was as the second-line act behind folksinger Richie Havens. Ironically, Havens was one of the musicians present at that first hearing of Jimi's English album. At the time he remarked, "Whew, I'd hate to have to follow that guy on the stage."

It was one of the hottest nights of the summer of 1967, and they were lined up around the block in front of the Cafe Au Go Go. The third act on the bill that night was a jazz-rock group led by flutist Jeremy Steig. They played a long and exciting set, but most of the crowd had come to hear the Experience. The club's air conditioner was broken, and the room was particularly hot and smokey. As Steig's people were clearing the stage, Jimi appeared with a can of room deodorant. "Pretty funky group," he said, as he proceeded to spray the stage.

The Experience played a set that night that may have been their best ever. A lot of well-known musicians were in the audience, and Jimi wanted to clearly establish his place as the "top cat." After an hour and a half Jimi said, "I'm feelin' pretty good, and I think I'll play all night. Any requests?"

After another overwhelming hour of music, the club's stage manager was desperately trying to signal the group to stop. It was after 3 A.M., and the headlined act, Richie

Havens, still had to do his set. But Hendrix ignored these signals, and kept playing and playing. Finally, at about 4 A.M., the management threatened to cut off the electricity. Jimi went into his usual guitar-breaking routine. But this time, he pounded the ceiling of the stage with a vengeance.

As the group left the stage, their amplifiers were still blasting while concrete and dust were descending from the ceiling. Everyone in that room fully understood why the group was called the Experience. As for poor Richie Havens, he knew better than to try to perform his usual set. Instead, he put on a record of the Beatles' "With a Little Help from My Friends," and urged the crowd to sing along. Everyone responded willingly. We were all in need of some light relief after what we had just witnessed.

Jimi was now a star. His first album quickly reached the top five, and his group could demand top billing wherever it performed. Unlike most rock superstars, Hendrix was always accessible to his fans. When asked to "party," Jimi rarely said no in those days. Local musicians found him ready to jam at almost any time of the night or day. By 1968, Jimi had conquered the rock scene on three fronts: he was clearly its most inspired musician; he was its wildest and most uninhibited performer, and he was the loudest, and most offensive symbol that the flower-power world of rock could throw in the face of the straitlaced adult world. Although his wild image and performing antics brought him the greatest amount of publicity, it was his musical genius that secures his position as one of rock's all-time greats.

Jimi showed another side of that genius on his second album, *Axis: Bold as Love*. Although this album was recorded only a few weeks after *Are You Experienced*, much of the music has a completely different flavor. On songs like "Little Wing," and "Castles Made of Sand," Hendrix displayed his more delicate and poetic side. Even on these songs, he used feedback and other electronic devices. But he seemed to have complete control over what was happening in his music. On his first two albums, Jimi had covered a wide musical range which included blues, soul, psychedelic sounds, and jazz improvisation. Furthermore, he freely could mix these styles, producing results that were uniquely his own.

But Jimi did not seem to be particularly impressed with his own musicianship. He often spoke of sounds in his head that he could not play. These frustrations could often be seen in his live performances. He wanted, but never did receive, the full acceptance of black audiences. Hendrix also felt insecure about his standing among jazz musicians. He often asked, "What do these cats think of me, do they think I'm jiving?"

By the latter part of 1968, Jimi's personal problems became more visible. His performances lost much of their magic as he began relying more on visual tricks. He felt contempt when audiences were fooled by this trickery and seemed to have the attitude that there was nothing left to prove. Also, there were rumors of dissension within the group, particularly between Jimi and bassist Noel Redding. These rumors were fueled when Hendrix's third album featured bassist Billy Cox and drummer Buddy Miles on a number of the cuts.

The new album featured several exceptional songs, including the title cut, "Electric Ladyland," "Crosstown Traffic," and "Voodoo Chile." The last song contained a lineup of Stevie Winwood on organ, Jack Cassidy of the Jefferson Airplane on bass, and Buddy Miles on drums. The song is a powerful restatement of the Muddy Waters' classic "Hoochie Koochie Man." It stands as Hendrix's ultimate achievement as a blues guitarist.

In early 1969, the Experience disbanded. Jimi then entered a period of personal decline which ended with his death the following year. In May, Jimi was arrested at Toronto's International Airport for possession of heroin. He was eventually found innocent, on the basis of his claim that he was given an envelope by a fan, but did not know what it contained. Nevertheless, Jimi's taste for drugs was legend in music circles.

Shortly after the Toronto "bust," Jimi was scheduled to appear on a television show with Steven Stills and the Jefferson Airplane. At the halfway point in the program, Jimi had still not arrived. When the show's host asked Stills as to Hendrix's whereabouts, he replied: "Jimi is still in the motel room; he was just too stoned to leave."

During the summer of 1969, Jimi rented a big house in Woodstock and filled it with a group of musicians ranging from blues guitarists to avant-garde classical and jazz composers. He wanted to work with different kinds of musicians and experiment in different musical styles. He called this gathering an "electric sky church." Although some of these musicians appeared with him at the Woodstock festival, Hendrix never really got the group off the ground.

Next he organized a new all-black trio with Buddy Miles and Billy Cox called Band of Gypsies. The group recorded an album and seemed to have the potential of surpassing the Experience. But Jimi wasn't strong enough to keep the unit together. During a peace benefit at Madison Square Garden, Hendrix stopped playing in the middle of a set and just walked off the stage. A short time later, Band of Gypsies disbanded.

Shortly thereafter, the original Experience re-formed. But in a few weeks, they broke up again. Hendrix did some performing with Mitchell and Cox and some jamming in his recently completed studio in New York — Electric Ladyland. During the early part of 1970, he played a festival at the Isle of Wight and then toured Europe. These were to be his final performances.

Jimi Hendrix died in his sleep in the apartment of a girl friend on September 18, 1970. The official cause of death was "from inhalation of vomit following barbiturate intoxication." According to the girl friend, Hendrix had taken a large number of sleeping pills. The coroner could not reach a definite verdict as to whether the death was caused by suicide or accident. In any case, it seemed clearly related to drug abuse.

The question of why so many rock stars die prematurely is a difficult one to answer. In Hendrix's case, we get a picture of a man who could not deal with the pressures of stardom. On one hand, he was a musical genius. But on the other hand, he was insecure about his talent. He often resorted to tricks while he was performing, but hated the audience for responding to these gimmicks. He always had a lot of people around him, but apparently lacked close friends. One writer in *Rolling Stone* noted that all of the people who knew him gave different accounts of his feelings, his drug use, his attitudes about being black, and his relationship with his managers. The writer concludes: "Nobody with a vested interest seems to be able to speak authoritatively about Hendrix, and so his death has only deepened the mystery and confusion, only reinforced his image as a freak genius."

Since his death, there have been several attempts to release posthumous albums. Some of these contained musicians adding to tracks that Hendrix had recorded during the last few months of his life. Some of this music is better than one might expect, but none of it approaches the standard that was set on the first three albums.

Ten years have passed since Hendrix's death, and nobody has come close to duplicating the things he did with an electric guitar. In a way, it is unfortunate that people keep trying. When Hendrix changed the guitar from a mere musical instrument to an electric rocket, it unleashed the imaginations of thousands of lesser musicians. Their inept imitations sound like so much noise. Hendrix, of course, cannot be blamed for this. He never meant to pave the way for others. He must have known that the average player first has to master the techniques of playing his instrument before delving into electronics. But Jimi Hendrix was beyond questions of playing the guitar, or controlling electronic equipment. He wanted to "touch the sun," and "kiss the sky. . . ." Ultimately, he did.

JIMI HENDRIX COLLECTORS' GUIDE

*— Smash Hit

ALBUMS

Year	Album	Label	Hit
1967	Are You Experienced	Reprise	*
1967	Get That Feeling (w/Curtis Knight)	Capitol	
1968	Axis: Bold as Love	Reprise	*
1968	Electric Ladyland	Reprise	*
1969	Smash Hits	Reprise	*
1970	Hendrix Band of Gypsies (w/Buddy Miles and Billy Cox)	Capitol	*
1971	The Cry of Love	Reprise	*
1971	Rainbow Bridge (Soundtrack)	Reprise	*
1971	Two Great Experiences Together (w/Lonnie Youngblood)	Maple	
1972	Hendrix in the West	Reprise	*
1972	Jimi Hendrix: War Heroes	Reprise	

Year	Album	Label	Hit
1972	*Rare Hendrix*	Trip	
1973	*Soundtrack Recordings from the film Jimi Hendrix*	Reprise	
1975	*Crash Landing*	Reprise	*
1975	*Midnight Lightning*	Reprise	
1980	*9 to the Universe*	Reprise	

SINGLES

Year	Single	Label	Hit
1967	*Hey Joe/51st Anniversary*	Reprise	*
1967	*Wind Cries Mary/Purple Haze*	Reprise	
1967	*Foxy Lady*	Reprise	
1968	*One Rainy Wish/Up From the Skies*	Reprise	
1968	*All Along the Watchtower/Burning of the Midnight Lamp*	Reprise	*
1968	*Crosstown Traffic/Gypsy Eyes*	Reprise	
1971	*Freedom*	Reprise	
1971	*Dolly Dagger*	Reprise	

Rock 'n' Roll Women

7. ARETHA FRANKLIN

ARETHA FRANKLIN is clearly the greatest female singer in the popular music field. She is blessed with a magnificently versatile and powerful voice, as well as an unmatched gift for improvisation. She has written a number of her own hit songs, but her great strength is interpreting the work of other writers. A few examples are: Carole King's "A Natural Woman," Paul Simon's "Bridge over Troubled Water," and Otis Redding's "Respect." When she sings these songs, Aretha adds her own emotional quality to them. It is almost as though she is rewriting melodies and even lyrics as she sings.

From the late sixties up until the middle seventies, Aretha won more Grammy Awards than any other female artist. Aretha was voted the top female artist by many music publications and even landed on the cover of both *Time* and *Newsweek* magazines. But the past few years have not been

145

Aretha Franklin—a
once-in-a-lifetime talent
Record World—Atlantic Records

especially kind to Aretha. Even her most devoted fans have come away disappointed from her recent concerts. She seems to be going through a period of confusion, both emotional and artistic. Her performances contain too many soft ballads instead of the fire-charged music that stirred her admirers to crown her "The Queen of Soul."

Because of her boundless talent, Aretha must be considered an artist who has not achieved her potential. But on the other hand, how do you improve on records like "Never Loved a Man," "Respect," and "Chain of Fools"? An even more fascinating question is how did the lady develop the talent to sing like that?

She always seemed destined for a life in music. Her father, the Reverend C. L. Franklin, was one of the most well respected and successful gospel ministers in America. As the head of Detroit's New Bethel Baptist Church, Reverend Franklin became the major figure in that city's gospel community. Many famous gospel artists stayed at the Franklin home whenever they were in town. With encouragement from people like James Cleveland, Mahalia Jackson, and Clara Ward, young Aretha became a gospel star in her own right. She made her first public appearance at the funeral of a relative, joining the Clara Ward Singers in a moving rendition of "Peace in the Valley." Shortly thereafter, Aretha began recording gospel music for the Chess label. She had not yet reached her fourteenth birthday.

In spite of her early success, Aretha did not have a particularly happy childhood. In describing her teenage years, writer Arnold Shaw notes: "Aretha was a nice girl, but also a troubled girl. Growing up in a middle-class ghetto just outside of the poor black neighborhood that nourished Diana Ross and other Motown artists, she missed both maternal and paternal love."

Aretha's mother left the family when she was six, and died when the young girl was ten. This seemed to have a profound effect on all the Franklins. During the next few years, Aretha performed as a featured singer with her father on the gospel circuit. Life on the road was a grueling ordeal. Most of her formative years were spent traveling from town to town, often sleeping in the back seats of cars.

As Aretha's older brother and manager explained to a reporter from *Time* magazine, "Driving eight to ten hours trying to make a gig, being hungry and passing restaurants along the road, and having to go off the highway into some little city to find a place to eat because you're black — that had its effect." The *Time* article also notes that "the postperformance parties among older troupers in hotel rooms where the liquor and sex were plentiful had their effect too."

By the time Aretha was eighteen, she was ready to give up her life on the gospel circuit and try her luck in the world of popular music. The great Sam Cooke, who had made the same transition several years earlier, encouraged Aretha to "make the move" as soon as possible. Cooke wanted Aretha to sign with his record label, RCA, but John Hammond was determined to sign her for Columbia. Hammond, who had worked with Billie Holliday and Bob Dylan, considered the young Aretha "an untutored genius." He strongly believed that under his influence, she would develop into the best singer in popular music. But Hammond could not achieve for Aretha what he did for others. In a 1976 interview with *Record World* magazine, Hammond discussed Aretha's years at Columbia and the reasons that she did not achieve stardom on that label:

That first session with Aretha was one of the most exciting sessions I've had in all my life. There were about six or seven guys in the band, no charts. Ray Bryant was the leader in some of the things and played piano, but in things like "Summertime," and "Today I Sing the Blues" it was Aretha who played piano. I knew I had probably the greatest singer since Billie Holliday, as far as my own experience in the studio was concerned.

Columbia was not geared to sell black records in those days. The stores that sold black records simply were not considered good credit risks. . . . I wanted Aretha to really make it in black radio and in black stores, and then we could build on that to get a wider market. But I didn't want in any way to try and make her a top forty artist, because this wasn't really her bag.

We made her first album which has now been reissued, called "Aretha Franklin — Her First Twelve Sides" and out of those twelve sides, there were four singles, all of which went over one hundred thousand, which was amazing for (a black record on) Columbia in those days. The album as such didn't sell too much. But she got some very good reviews.

And then politics began to enter the Columbia scene. In the summer of 1961 . . . (Columbia) had signed Al Kasha as

Aretha's producer for singles and I was to continue to produce Aretha for albums. This didn't work out at all. Al had a completely different idea, he wanted to make her a top forty artist. . . . The first thing we found was big band arrangements and strings and all the rest of the trappings of making a pop star out of a good soulful black girl. . . .

I stopped producing her. Bob Mersey and various other people made a lot of albums with Aretha, and they didn't have the same bite and excitement that I thought the original albums had. Aretha stayed at Columbia for five years, until 1966. She was never very comfortable with a jazz (or pop) background; Aretha always had to have a rock drummer — which is right. . . ."

By the end of her tenure at Columbia, Aretha was confused and depressed. During her five years there, she had gone through her paces and learned to sing virtually every kind of popular song. But she had not been allowed to sing the kind of music for which she was best suited. While other former gospel singers like Wilson Pickett and Sam and Dave were making million-selling records, Aretha was in debt to Columbia to the tune of ninety thousand dollars. When her contract with that label expired in 1966, she immediately signed a long-term agreement with producer Jerry Wexler of Atlantic Records. Within a year, she was the top singer in America, and her debt to Columbia had been completely wiped out.

Jerry Wexler described simply what he did for Aretha — "*I put her back in church.*" He hit on the one type of music which the producers at Columbia had neglected — funky, soulful, hard-hitting rhythm and blues. Wexler decided to record Aretha at Fame Studios in Muscle Shoals, Alabama. He knew that the musicians there thrived on her kind of music. Wexler centered the music around Aretha's voice and piano, as well as the background singing provided by her two sisters, Erma and Carolyn. The rest of the musicians quickly fell into place. The music that came out of these early Atlantic recordings represents Aretha at her best. In a recent conversation with *Record World* magazine, Wexler recalled these early sessions:

I thought Aretha had the best voice I'd ever heard in my life. . . . I never imagined I'd have the good luck to sign her. It was too good to be true. . . . I also didn't realize what a good piano player she was. And I started her playing a lot more piano on my records. . . .

She had a lot of songs for her first album. "I Never Loved a Man" (her first single and album) was written by Ronnie Shannon, a Detroit songwriter. She came in with that. She had the whole arrangement, and the whole idea of it, and it was just thrilling to hear. . . .

I thought "I Never Loved a Man" was an R&B hit. I was willing to settle for that for the first record, that would have been fine. . . . [The record eventually became a top ten pop hit.]

"Respect" was her next single. That was a Grammy winner. It was a pop record. I can't take any credit for that. She did it, she surprised me. She just went and did it. You'd never know. We would come in to the studio, and she would have six or eight songs all ready to go, and this was one. She'd have the layout, the piano part and the vocal backgrounds. So we just had to fill in the instruments — very little change.

I played a test of her version of "Respect" for Otis Redding (the song's composer who had recorded the original version). He said, "I just lost my song. That girl took it away from me." He said it in a spirit of generosity. He was thrilled with the record. And of course, it's the record that established him. Also, it's sort of the keynote record of the time. There were intimations of Women's Lib at the time. . . ."

Aretha maintained her momentum through her next four or five albums. She was one of the few soul artists to conceive entire albums. These records had a pace of their own, moving from uptempo dance numbers to stirring ballads with the greatest of ease. But by 1970, the popularity of soul music began to decline, and so did Aretha's creative energies. Meanwhile, she was becoming ever more absorbed by her personal problems.

Although she was now an adult with three children of her own, Aretha had never gotten over the pain of her troubled childhood. During an interview with *Time* magazine she confided, "I might be twenty-six, but I'm an old woman in disguise — twenty-six goin' on sixty-five. Trying to grow up is hurting, you know. You make mistakes. You try to learn from them, and when you don't it hurts even more. And I've been hurt, hurt bad."

As a number of her original songs reveal, much of Aretha's pain has come from an unsuccessful search for love. Her marriage to former manager Ted White ended terribly. There were even several incidents during which Aretha was "publicly roughed up" by White. But intense personal pain is sometimes the catalyst which helps an artist create.

For a time, Aretha channeled her problems creatively. She turned her attentions more toward more sensitive and soul-searching material. Songs like "I Say a Little Prayer," and "You're All I Need to Get By" show Aretha's more delicate side in a good light. But she also seemed to be reaching for new acceptance. Many of her records reverted back to the strings and lush orchestras of her early days at Columbia. At the same time, mediocre (for her) versions of songs like "Eleanor Rigby," and "The Weight" seemed designed to capture the white rock audience. But in 1971, the rock fans at San Francisco's Fillmore West showed that they could appreciate the real Aretha. As Jerry Wexler recalls:

I went into the Fillmore with great trepidation, wondering what we were going to get from people who were raised on the Grateful Dead and Jefferson Airplane. But Bill Graham (owner of the Fillmore) had the right idea. It became apparent that these people were really ready for Aretha; they responded to the right things in the music, and it was a very good audience. . . . Aretha just loved the audience. She loved being out there and was conscious now that she was finding a new audience. . . .

The result of that concert was a splendid album — *Live at the Fillmore West*. Aretha and her backup band, King Curtis and the Kingpins, were in top form. Toward the end of the concert, the great Ray Charles joined Aretha for a duet. A glowing Aretha told the cheering crowd, "You have been more to me than anything I could have expected."

From that point on, listeners never knew what to expect from an Aretha Franklin record. She recorded in a number of styles with widely variable results. In 1972, for example, Aretha won Grammys for two completely different kinds of albums.

Her first album that year, *Young Gifted and Black*, explores black pride and features a cover picture of Aretha in a natural hairdo and African clothes. A number of critics consider this album to be one of her best. In any case, Aretha seemed to be more concerned with exploring her feelings about being black. As she told a reporter from *Ebony* magazine: "I believe that the Black Revolution certainly forced me and the majority of black people to begin taking a second look at ourselves. It wasn't that we were all that ashamed of ourselves, we merely started appreciating our natural selves. . . . Mine was a very personal evolution of the *me* in myself."

Aretha's second award winning album in 1972, *Amazing*

Grace, was a return to her own personal roots in the black church. The record, which features James Cleveland, was a spiritual and musical triumph. Surprisingly, this gospel album found its way to the top ten album charts.

After *Amazing Grace,* Aretha began to return to records which featured lush arrangements and a soft beat. Once again, she seemed to be trying to woo the "sophisticated" supper club audience. She had a number of hits in the mid-seventies including: "Until You Come Back to Me," "I'm In Love," and "Mr. D.J." For the most part, these records did not reach the high standards which she had set. During recent years, the quality and success of Aretha's work has trailed off even more.

Any discussion of Aretha's decline must take her enormous talent into consideration. A mediocre Aretha Franklin record still overshadows the best work of most other singers. Still, it is distressing to see Aretha on the Dick Clark show, dressed like an Egyptian princess, singing a syrupy rendition of "You Light Up My Life." Perhaps, as some people have suggested, Aretha does not appreciate her own talent. But then again, one must ask if the world truly appreciates how great an artist Aretha Franklin is.

Rhythm and blues is one of the more neglected and unappreciated art forms. Aretha has as much technique as *any* singer, plus an emotional range and ability to improvise that have never been matched by a popular vocalist. She is truly a talent which comes along once in a lifetime.

Over the years, the world of rock has lost many of its greatest performers. Thankfully, Aretha is still with us. Furthermore, she has lost little of her ability to sing. Occasionally she will appear on TV and "get it on" as only she can. Those of us who appreciate her genius can only hope that she regains her creative spark and assumes her rightful place as the greatest vocal talent of her time.

ARETHA FRANKLIN COLLECTORS' GUIDE
* — *Smash Hit*

ALBUMS

Year	Album	Label	Hit
1960	*Gospel Soul*	Checker	
1961	*Aretha*	Columbia	
1961	*Electrifying Aretha Franklin*	Columbia	
1962	*The Tender, The Moving, The Swinging Aretha Franklin*	Columbia	
1963	*Laughing on the Outside*	Columbia	
1964	*Unforgettable*	Columbia	
1964	*Songs of Faith*	Columbia	
1964	*Runnin' Out of Fools*	Columbia	
1965	*Yeah*	Columbia	
1966	*Soul Sister*	Columbia	
1967	*Take It Like You Give It*	Columbia	
1967	*Aretha Franklin's Greatest Hits*	Columbia	
1967	*I Never Loved a Man*	Atlantic	*
1967	*Aretha Arrives*	Atlantic	*
1967	*Take a Look*	Columbia	
1968	*Aretha Franklin's Greatest Hits*	Columbia	
1968	*Aretha: Lady Soul*	Atlantic	*
1968	*Aretha Now*	Atlantic	*
1968	*Aretha in Paris*	Atlantic	*
1969	*Aretha Franklin Soul '69*	Atlantic	*
1969	*Aretha's Gold*	Atlantic	*
1970	*This Girl's in Love with You*	Atlantic	*
1970	*Spirit in the Dark*	Atlantic	
1971	*Aretha Live at Fillmore West*	Atlantic	*
1971	*Aretha's Greatest Hits*	Atlantic	*

Year	Album	Label	Hit
1972	*Young Gifted and Black*	Atlantic	*
1972	*Amazing Grace (w/James Cleveland)*	Atlantic	*
1972	*In the Beginning/The World of Aretha Franklin 1960–1967*	Columbia	
1973	*Hey Now Hey*	Atlantic	
1973	*The First Twelve Sides*	Columbia	
1974	*Let Me in Your Life*	Atlantic	*
1974	*With Everything I Feel in Me*	Atlantic	
1975	*You*	Atlantic	
1976	*Sparkle*	Atlantic	
1976	*Ten Years of Gold*	Atlantic	*
1977	*Sweet Passion*	Atlantic	
1978	*Almighty Fire*	Atlantic	

SINGLES

Year	Single	Label	Hit
1960	*Today I Sing the Blues*	Columbia	
1961	*Won't Be Long*	Columbia	
1961	*Operation Heartache*	Columbia	
1962	*I Surrender Dear*	Columbia	
1962	*Rough Lover*	Columbia	
1962	*Don't Cry Baby*	Columbia	
1962	*Try a Little Tenderness*	Columbia	
1962	*Trouble in Mind*	Columbia	
1964	*Precious Lord (2 parts)*	Columbia	
1964	*Runnin' Out of Fools*	Columbia	
1965	*One Step Ahead*	Columbia	
1967	*I Never Loved a Man the Way I Do You*	Atlantic	*
1967	*Lee Cross*	Columbia	
1967	*Respect*	Atlantic	*

Year	Album	Label	Hit
1967	*Follow Your Heart/Take a Look*	Columbia	
1967	*Mother's Love/Mockingbird*	Columbia	
1967	*Baby I Love You*	Atlantic	*
1967	*A Natural Woman*	Atlantic	*
1967	*Chain of Fools*	Atlantic	*
1968	*Soulville*	Columbia	
1968	*(Sweet Baby Baby) Since You've Been Gone*	Atlantic	*
1968	*Think*	Atlantic	*
1968	*House That Jack Built*	Atlantic	*
1968	*See Saw*	Atlantic	*
1969	*The Weight*	Atlantic	*
1969	*I Can't See Myself Leaving You*	Atlantic	
1969	*Share Your Love with Me*	Atlantic	*
1969	*Eleanor Rigby*	Atlantic	*
1970	*Call Me*	Atlantic	*
1970	*Spirit in the Dark*	Atlantic	*
1970	*Border Song (Holy Moses)*	Atlantic	
1971	*You're All I Need to Get By*	Atlantic	*
1971	*Bridge over Troubled Water*	Atlantic	*
1971	*Spanish Harlem*	Atlantic	*
1971	*Rock Steady*	Atlantic	*
1972	*Oh Me Oh My (I'm a Fool for You Baby)*	Atlantic	
1972	*Day Dreaming*	Atlantic	*
1972	*All the Kings Horses*	Atlantic	
1973	*Master of Eyes*	Atlantic	
1973	*Angel*	Atlantic	*
1973	*Until You Come Back to Me (That's What I'm Gonna Do)*	Atlantic	*
1974	*I'm in Love*	Atlantic	*
1974	*Ain't Nothing But the Real Thing Baby*	Atlantic	
1974	*Without Love*	Atlantic	
1975	*With Everything I Feel in Me*	Atlantic	
1975	*Mr. D.J. (5 for the D.J.)*	Atlantic	

Year	Album	Label	Hit
1976	*Something He Can Feel*	Atlantic	
1976	*Jump*	Atlantic	
1976	*Break It to Me Gently*	Atlantic	
1977	*Meadows of Springtime*	Atlantic	
1978	*Almighty Fire (Woman of the Future)*	Atlantic	

Rock 'n' Roll Women

8. JANIS JOPLIN

"I gotta go on doin' it the way I see it. . . . I got no choice but to take it like I see it. I'm here to have a party while I'm on this earth. . . . I'm gettin' it now, today. I don't even know where I'm gonna be twenty years from now, so I'm just gonna keep on rockin', cause if I start saving up bits and pieces of me . . . man, there ain't gonna be nothing left for Janis. — Janis Joplin, 1967 (excerpt from David Dalton's *Janis*)

ALTHOUGH JANIS JOPLIN is generally acknowledged to be the most important white female singer in rock history, her personality has left a greater impact than her music. As the first woman to achieve the status of a full-fledged rock superstar, Janis displayed a degree of personal and musical freedom that few others would ever attempt to duplicate. Nevertheless, many women — both in and out of music — were encouraged to take greater risks in their own lives.

Janis would never come out and declare herself on the side of women's liberation. She wasn't the type to carry a banner for any cause. When asked about the growing feminist movement, she would coyly answer: "I'm for equal

158

Janis Joplin—spilling out her guts, exposing her pain, and laying her soul bare.
Record World—Columbia Records

rights, and equal pay, and all that crap. But I don't want dudes to stop opening the door for me."

At other times, however, Janis indicated that she wanted to be a force in bringing about social change. "People aren't supposed to be like me," she would often say. "They're not supposed to sing like me, drink like me, or live like me. But now they're paying me 100 thousand dollars a year to be like me. That's what I hope I mean to those kids out there. After they see me — when their mothers are feeding them all that cashmere girdle bull — maybe they'll have second thoughts that they can be themselves and win."

At the time of this statement, Janis had already been on the cover of almost every national magazine. But it hadn't always been that way. Her childhood years were terribly unhappy. She had grown up in the small Texas town of Port Arthur during the fifties, the oldest child of an oil refinery executive. In an era that prized conformity above all else, Janis found herself unable to fit in. She didn't look right, didn't talk right, and had ideas that seemed crazy to those around her.

"I always wanted to be an artist like other chicks wanted to be stewardesses," she told an interviewer from *Crawdaddy*. "Port Arthur people thought I was a beatnik, and they didn't like beatniks — though they had never seen one and neither had I. I read, I painted, I thought, I didn't hate blacks. There was nobody like me in Port Arthur. It was lonely, those feelings welling up inside and nobody to talk to. I was just silly, crazy Janis. Man, those people really hurt me. . . ."

Like the blues artists she so greatly admired, Janis found out early that music was one of the only real outlets for her pain. As a young girl, she learned to sing hillbilly and traditional folk music. By the time she entered college in the early sixties, she was a fairly accomplished blues singer. Her main influences back in those days were Bessie Smith and Leadbelly. But she didn't really develop her own style until she came to San Francisco and joined the rock group *Big Brother and the Holding Company*.

The year was 1966, and San Francisco's Haight-Ashbury district was the center of a growing movement. The hippie culture was getting itself together, with rock music and psychedelic drugs as its mainstays. Big Brother was one of many local bands that were forming around that time. As it happened, they were looking for a girl singer. Travis Rivers — an old drinking buddy of Janis's from Texas — knew that she would be perfect for the band. He immediately returned to Port Arthur, and convinced Janis to leave college — he didn't really have to be all that persuasive. Within days, they were both on their way to San Francisco.

From her very first rehearsal with Big Brother, Janis knew that she would have to find a new way of singing. Somehow she had to make her voice stand out above the group's loud amplifiers and drums. "It was the most thrilling time in my life," Janis told *Crawdaddy*. "I couldn't believe it, all that rhythm and power. I got stoned just feeling it, like it was the best dope in the world. It was so sensual, so vibrant, loud, and crazy, that I couldn't stay still. I had never danced when I sang, but there I was moving and jumping. I couldn't hear myself, so I sang louder and louder. And by the end, I was wild."

At that moment, Janis actually invented a new style of rock 'n' roll singing that was totally her own. With her up front, Big Brother became one of Haight Ashbury's top three bands along with the Jefferson Airplane and the Grateful Dead. In the spring of 1967, Big Brother was still a San Francisco phenomenon, although there was some talk in music business circles about a San Francisco band with a "fantastic chick singer." But by the end of that summer, Janis Joplin had become a household word.

The Monterey Pop Festival, held in June 1967, was much more than Janis's introduction to the national audience. All things considered, it probably marked the high point of her career. As she screamed, hollered, and pleaded her way through Big Mamma Thornton's "Ball and Chain," a stunned audience held its collective breath. When she finally cried out the last agonizing notes of a song, the huge crowd went berserk. Nobody had ever heard anyone sing with this much intensity. Everything about Janis's body movements and facial expressions told you that this was much more than a great performance. Rather, this was a real flesh and blood woman, spilling out her guts, exposing her pain, and laying her soul bare.

Janis had often said that there was no difference between the way she sang and the way she lived. The pain and guilt she had carried with her since childhood were right there in her performance. The frantic way that she moved her body and shrieked through her songs scarcely covered up the screams of a love-starved child. Underneath all the shouting and pounding, there was a scared little girl who was crying out for help.

Unfortunately, the love of her audiences did little to soothe Janis's pain. The loneliness which haunted her personal life stood in bitter contrast to the love her fans showered upon her. Janis had a number of remedies for her suffering. Most of them were self-destructive.

Janis's sexual exploits have always been an important part of her legend. Although she never had what most people would call a genuine love relationship, she certainly did have lovers. Janis liked to pick up "pretty young boys," and compete with the male band members' exploits with female groupies. People who knew her well felt that although Janis often bragged about her sexual conquests, she really didn't get much satisfaction from this part of her life. On the other hand, Janis seemed to get much more pleasure from her music. "Singing is more to me than sex," she often said. "When I sing, I feel chills and weird feelings slipping all over my body. To me, it's a supreme emotional and physical experience."

As ecstatic as her singing made her feel, Janis needed to muster a great deal of courage simply to walk out on stage. It is no secret that she often drank heavily before a performance. But Janis's drinking never worried anybody too much. It was just another part of her myth which she discussed as freely as her sex life. Loving fans presented her with bottles, and everybody thought it was a big joke. So what if Janis was always drunk? After all, alcohol is a legal drug. It is the same drug that many business people and politicians take with their lunch. So Janis made no secret of her heavy drinking, even if it was destroying her. She openly went on binges in full view of anyone who happened to be around. She was, however, far more secretive about another of her habits — shooting heroin.

When people talk about the San Francisco rock scene in the 1960's, they always mention psychedelic music and psychedelic drugs. LSD is the drug that most of the musicians were experimenting with in those days, but not Janis. The last thing she wanted was a drug that would heighten her emotions. The drugs Janis took were those which helped her escape from her problems. No other substance accomplished this for her as well as heroin. She first picked up the needle soon after her triumph at Monterey. Apparently, her growing fame was making her anxious, and she needed something to "slow her down." And while Janis wasn't the only member of Big Brother who used the drug, she was by far the least discreet.

With all of the partying, drinking, and shooting up, Janis never really paid that much attention to her music. Basically, she was a singer who needed to be seen in order to be fully appreciated. "If I were a musician it might be a lot harder to get all that feeling out," she told writer Ralph J. Gleason. "But I'm fortunate because my gig is just closing my eyes and feeling things." Janis's lack of polish was obvious on Big Brother's first album — Cheap Thrills. But the rock press blamed the musicians for all the record's shortcomings.

"It's true that we were a bunch of amateurs who played out of tune," Big Brother drummer Dave Getz admits. "But Janis was an amateur too. She was better than the rest of us, but not really that much better." Nevertheless, the word among rock critics was, "Janis is the greatest. Big Brother, the lowest." By the fall of 1968, the group had lost its "fantastic chick singer."

Janis had always idolized great rhythm and blues performers like Otis Redding, James Brown, and Tina Turner.

She longed to be considered on a par with these great artists, though she lacked their polish. Still, she wanted to try to put together the same kind of band that most of the R&B singers had. So, she hired a group of experienced back-up musicians to replace Big Brother. This meant that she now kept the lion's share of the money, while the musicians were paid a weekly salary. She was the leader of the band and supposedly in complete control of the music. But Janis

Big Brother and the Holding Company—a musical family that sometimes played out of tune
Record World—Columbia Records

soon learned that there was a big difference between cooperating with a group of equal partners and whipping a bunch of hired hands into shape.

Big Brother and the Holding Company may not have been the world's greatest musicians, but they were a real band. The group had come up together, and they thought of themselves as an organic unit. Only a few months before Janis left the group, writer Richard Goldstein described the relationship between Janis and Big Brother this way: "From the start, their music began to clothe her voice. They taught her to blast, pound, and shatter a song. She returned the favor by directing her solos inward, toward the group's rhythmic heart. In fact, Janis had made her voice into a family. It shows. People think of Big Brother and the Holding Company as a family."

But now, the family was gone. Janis was on her own. Her performances with the new band did not electrify the crowds. Janis seemed less spontaneous, and her audiences often became restless. No longer did they "freak out" after each number and demand three and four encores. Janis often had to command them to respond. "Why the hell don't you get off your butts and dance?" she would rasp.

Meanwhile, the rock press did a complete turnabout. They pleaded with Janis to return to Big Brother, *if* they would have her. In a review of her first San Francisco concert with the new band, Ralph J. Gleason wrote: "Her new band is a drag. They can play OK but they are a pale version of the Memphis-Detroit bands from the rhythm and blues shows . . . Janis, though in good voice, seems bent on becoming Aretha Franklin. The best things they did were most like her songs with Big Brother. . . ."

In spite of all the problems, Janis's one album with her second band did have some good moments. *Got Them Old Kozmic Blues Again* was a more well-crafted album than her work with Big Brother. Guitarist Sam Andrew — the one member of Big Brother who accompanied Janis in her next band — felt that Janis wanted to see if she could cut it with a soul band. The group did a European tour, and things definitely improved. But the combination never quite jelled. By the end of 1969, Janis's second band — which never had an official name — was no more.

The last few months of Janis's life were full of contradictions. In many ways, it appeared as if she were finally getting herself together. She had formed a new group — Full Tilt Boogie — which was her best by far. The album they were working on — *Pearl* — was released shortly after Janis's death. Finally, Janis was singing with a maturity and control that had been missing throughout her career. She had even met a man whom she intended to marry, although these plans seemed somewhat vague.

Many of Janis's friends stated that they had never seen her so happy. They discounted any possibility that she would have taken her own life. The fact that Janis had signed a new will just two days before her death was labeled a coincidence. On the other hand, she had recently been warned that her continued use of heroin would result in her death. As far as most of Janis's friends knew, she had been off the stuff for months. But lately, she had begun shooting up again. On the night of October 4, 1970, Janis Joplin was found dead in a lonely Los Angeles hotel room. The cause of death was an overdose of heroin. She was twenty-seven.

There has been much speculation about whether or not Janis's death was intentional. Given her self-destructive tendencies, it would be difficult to call her passing an accident. Janis's close friend and biographer, Myra Friedman, may have put it best when she wrote: "Chronic suicide is what Janis was engaged in throughout her life, the act taking this form or that along the way and penetrating all areas of her tortured existence."

There is something ironic in the timing of Janis's death, coming as it did at the beginning of the new decade. There were a number of other rock stars who died within a year of Janis: Jimi Hendrix, whom she considered her cosmic twin; Brian Jones of the Rolling Stones, and Jim Morrison of the Doors. The lifestyles as well as the deaths of these performers were remarkably similar to Janis's.

All of these artists belonged to an era so shattering that the world has still not recovered from its impact. Many of the events of the sixties are still not fully understood. But the influence of rock and certain rock musicians on those crucial years cannot be overestimated. As the most visible rock 'n' roll woman of her time — and perhaps of all time — Janis Joplin was more than just a symbol of the sixties. As much — and perhaps more than any of her contemporaries, she *was* the sixties.

JANIS JOPLIN COLLECTORS' GUIDE
— Smash Hit

ALBUMS

Year	Album	Label	Hit
1967	Big Brother and the Holding Company (w/Big Brother)	Mainstream	
1968	Cheap Thrills (w/Big Brother)	Columbia	*
1969	I Got Them Old Kozmic Blues Again	Columbia	*
1971	Pearl	Columbia	*
1972	Joplin in Concert	Columbia	*
1973	Janis Joplin's Greatest Hits	Columbia	

SINGLES

Year	Single	Label	Hit
1968	*All Is Loneliness/Blind Man*	Mainstream	
1968	*Bye Bye Baby/Intruder*	Mainstream	
1968	*Piece of My Heart*	Columbia	*
1968	*Down on Me*	Mainstream	
1968	*Coo Coo*	Mainstream	
1969	*Kozmic Blues*	Columbia	
1971	*Me and Bobby McGee*	Columbia	*
1971	*Get It While You Can*	Columbia	
1972	*Down on Me*	Columbia	

Rock 'n' Roll Women

9. DONNA SUMMER

"I can sing 'Love to Love You Baby,' but I can sing ballads . . . church hymns, all kinds of songs. Plus, I can write, act, and think. I'm multidimensional, and I don't want to be known for just one thing." (*Ebony* Magazine)

SHE IS the reigning queen of disco and one of the most successful performers in the business. But the question is — can we call her music "rock?"

Back in the 1950's, kids used to rate new records on Dick Clark's *American Bandstand*. "I'll give it a nine," they would say. "It's got a good beat; you can dance to it." More than the melody or the lyrics, rock 'n' roll has always been characterized by its beat — *the big beat.*

Before Alan Freed and other white disc jockeys began calling it rock 'n' roll, the music was called rhythm and blues. This was the popular music that black people listened to *and danced to.* There were a number of authentic R&B styles back then, including New Orleans dance blues and Chicago rhythm and blues. There were definite differences among the various types of R&B. The New Orleans style usually featured chugging horn lines, while the Chicago style favored guitars. But there was one thing that all R&B had in common — *a strong dance beat.*

Throughout the 1950's, teenagers of all races listened and danced to the *big beat.* Suddenly in 1961, the twist became an international dance craze among adults as well as kids. In reality, there was nothing new about the twist. It had the same beat as hundreds of other fast rhythm and blues songs. Nevertheless, the dance became the hottest fad of the early 1960's.

In order to accommodate the thousands of dancers who wanted to dance the twist, hundreds of discotheques began springing up in major cities everywhere. The most famous of these was New York's Peppermint Lounge. While the house band — Joey Dee and the Starlighters — played "The Peppermint Twist," well-known celebrities were slipping

Donna Summer—the hottest singer around
Record World—Casablanca Records

doormen five and ten dollar bills just to be let on the crowded dance floor. These famous personalities included Ambassador Adlai Stevenson, the Duke of Bedford, and playright Tennessee Williams. Soon millions of formerly square adults were dancing the twist.

To the serious rock fan, the twist craze marked the end of an era, the beat had become so important that record companies were ignoring everything else about the music's character. And so there were many bad singers recording uninspired songs in those days. As a result, serious listeners began turning away from rock 'n' roll to folk music and jazz.

This all changed again in the middle and late sixties. The Beatles, Dylan, the Stones, and others had made rock a formidable music again. In fact, their music was so good that most people preferred to listen rather than dance. At the same time, however, a number of important black artists were creating a new kind of rhythm and blues — *soul music.*

Several astute record producers had succeeded in combining the beat of traditional R&B with the spirit and vocal harmonies of black gospel music. To this combination, they added a wealth of recording techniques and much of the slickness of pop music. Disco is an outgrowth of this music.

Listen to a James Brown record from that era such as "Cold Sweat," "Say It Loud," "Mother Popcorn," or a dozen others. This is clearly some of the greatest dance music of our age. Listen also to the records of Sly and The Family Stone, and Motown artists like The Four Tops. The guts of the disco sound — the drum and bass parts — are right there. Even closer to the disco sound are some of the Philadelphia soul records of the early seventies, especially producer Willie Mitchell's work with singer Al Green. Songs like "Let's Stay Together," "I Want to Be with You," and almost every other tune on *Al Green's Greatest Hits* album has the same beat as most disco records. Still, critics do not consider Green a disco artist. His music may have the right beat, but it doesn't have the *disco attitude.*

Where then does all of this leave Donna Summer? For one thing, she is probably the single person most responsible for defining the disco attitude. Her seventeen-minute version of "Love to Love You, Baby," released in 1975, became the anthem for the new disco craze. On this record, Donna's European producers provided a lush track, a hypnotic beat, and the atmosphere of a sci-fi movie. And riding over it all was Donna singing only the title line: "Ooh, love to love you, baby." But as Donna moaned, and groaned, and cooed, there was no doubt about what was taking place. Her producers were casting Donna not as a singer, but as a sexual prop. Donna was not very happy about her new image, but she wasn't going to complain too strenuously. She understood how difficult it was to get that first hit.

When Donna Gaines left her Boston home at eighteen to accept a part in the Munich company of *Hair,* she didn't think she would have to wait eight years for her first hit. During that time, she had married a German actor named Helmut Sommer and had a daughter. When the marriage broke up, Donna retained an Americanized version of her ex-husband's name. After *Hair* closed, Donna got work in the Vienna Folk Opera productions of *Showboat* and *Porgy and Bess.* Although she was making a decent living, Donna had no intention of pursuing a career as a theatrical singer.

Whenever she had the time, Donna would sing backup at Munich's Musicland Studios. There were a number of producers at the studio who were experimenting with a new sound called Eurodisco. Among them were Giorgio Moroder and Pete Bellotte who owned the Munich-based Oasis Label. After Donna signed with Moroder and Bellotte, she wrote and recorded several songs which became minor hits in some European cities.

In early 1975 Donna recorded a three-minute version of "Love to Love You, Baby." The record was popular in Paris, but flopped in other European cities. Around this time, Moroder and Bellotte leased the Oasis Label to an American company — Neil Bogart's Casablanca Records. When Bogart played "Love to Love You, Baby," for friends at a party, they kept requesting that he put it on over and over again. He quickly decided to ask Moroder and Bellotte for a seventeen-minute version of the song to take up a full side of Donna's first album.

Bogart decided to launch the song on two fronts. He got a number of radio shows to program the record after midnight, announcing it as, "seventeen minutes of love with Donna Summer." He also made sure that all of the important discos got a copy. That was really where the record belonged — in places where people danced for hours on end, hoping the music would never stop. This kind of frantic, non-stop dancing has always been particularly big in clubs frequented by homosexuals. Within a week, the album sold 40,000 copies in New York. Six weeks later, almost one-half million copies had been sold.

Donna still hadn't left Europe. She knew her record was a hit, but she had no idea of how popular she actually had become. When she returned to America, she was shocked to find hundreds of screaming fans waiting at the airport to greet her. Suddenly the long struggle was over. Donna's record was at the top of the charts. But all of these new fans weren't looking at Donna Summer as a good singer. To them she was the sex-queen of the disco.

As the lives of many superstars reveal, sudden fame and fortune does not always bring happiness. In Donna's case, it almost brought on a nervous breakdown. All of a sudden, there was just too much going on. She wasn't ready for all the demands placed on a superstar, and she wasn't particularly happy about being a sex-goddess. Soon Donna developed an ulcer. At one point, she was so distraught that she even forgot her name. With time, she has learned to handle the pressures of her enormous success. But sometimes she still fears losing control of her emotions.

One thing that has helped keep Donna together is her confidence in herself. She has no doubts about her musical talent. This positive attitude goes back to her early years. "Even as a child, I knew I was going to be something," she recently told *Penthouse* magazine. "I think I grew up with a very good outlook on who I was, who I was supposed to be. . . . There were times when my girl friends would all be going to school with new skirts, new this, new that and I didn't have anything new. . . . But I never envied them. . . . I didn't care because I knew I was going somewhere in my life."

In spite of all her self-confidence, Donna's childhood wasn't particularly happy. Donna Andrea Gaines was one of seven children growing up in a racially mixed area of Boston. Both parents worked, and the family wasn't really poor. Donna's mother was a school teacher, and her father worked at various jobs — including butcher, electrician, and janitor — in order to make ends meet. Donna characterizes her family life as noisy and competitive. And the racial tensions she encountered in school didn't make *that* experience very enjoyable.

Donna cannot remember a time in her life that she wasn't singing. Like many great black singers, she began singing gospel music in church at a very young age. She would often lock herself in her parents' bedroom and sing along with the records of Mahalia Jackson, the most beloved gospel singer of her time. Naturally, Donna also had her ear glued to the radio, listening to popular performers like Dinah Washington, and Diana Ross.

During her junior year in high school, Donna joined a

rock group called Crow. She was the only female, and the only black person in the band. By the time the group made its professional debut at Boston's Psychedelic Supermarket, Donna was heavily involved with drugs. She refers to this time in her life as her "Janis Joplin period." As the female lead singer of a rock band in 1967, it probably wasn't very difficult for Donna to assume that role. "It was that whole psychedelic period when everyone was trying and testing new things, and I just went overboard," she recalled in *Penthouse*. "I finally went so far that when I was eighteen I said — 'Enough!' God did not intend me to live my life this way!' And so I quit abruptly after two years, and I really haven't indulged in drugs since."

Nine years passed since that time, and Donna had come a long way. She was intelligent enough to know that getting to the top is not the hardest part of the battle. Hundreds of performers have reached the top of the charts and then faded from sight. The toughest trick in the music business is staying on top. Donna resolved that she would achieve this goal. In order to do this, it would be necessary to go beyond her image of the sighing, moaning, disco goddess. This did not mean she was planning to play down her sex appeal — not by a long shot. Donna's idea was to build her reputation as a talented and versatile singer.

During the past few years, Donna has grown tremendously as an artist. *Rolling Stone* called her two 1978 albums — *I Remember Yesterday* and *Once Upon a Time* "ambitious departures from the sexy marionette image and breathy vocal mannerisms that at times suspended disco's influence altogether." On *I Remember Yesterday*, Donna displayed an unusual mastery of pop styles, from romantic ballads to show style jazz numbers.

Once Upon a Time was written as a Cinderella-type fairy tale by Donna's producers. The story, which is loosely based on Donna's childhood, was the first product that she really identified with. The album is really more a statement of Moroder and Bellotte's electronic wizardry than a showcase for Donna's talents. Nevertheless, Donna has often expressed the desire to perform this disco-opera on the Broadway stage.

"There are 101 reasons why 1978 has been a terrific year for me," Donna told *People* magazine. Aside from the two albums, there was her first movie role in the disco-film *Thank God It's Friday.* There were two more number-one singles — "Last Dance," and "MacArthur Park." Finally, there was her first live album — *Live and More* — which clearly established her as one of the best female singers around.

At the age of thirty, Donna finally received the critical acceptance she had strived for. The *New York Daily News* summed up Donna's talent this way:

> Summer can obviously do quite a bit more than gasp suggestively on record. She can sing disco or Gershwin, Judy Garland or Mahalia Jackson. Her versatility makes Linda Ronstadt and EmmyLou Harris sound old and tired; her continuing sex appeal makes Dolly Parton seem more overdone than she is.

But in spite of all her achievements, Donna hadn't really established herself as a rock performer. Even her best performances on *Live and More* held more appeal for disco and pop fans than for rock listeners. To a large extent, the rock audience was divided about their feelings toward disco. Some listeners felt that disco was unrelated to rock, while others believed that the two styles were not really so far apart. Then in the late seventies, several established rock artists succeeded in merging rock with disco.

Donna Summer—assuming a Marilyn Monroe pose
Record World—Casablanca Records

Whenever a craze becomes widespread, people inevitably try to jump on the bandwagon. Thus, almost every pop singer made a disco record in the late seventies. Even established rock stars like James Taylor and Paul McCartney have tried to go disco. For the most part, these records have little to recommend them. However, three established rock artists did manage to make authentic rock-disco crossovers: The Rolling Stones — "Miss You"; Rod Stewart — "Do You Think I'm Sexy," and Blondie — "Heart of Glass." These records were the first to be accepted as genuine rock by rock fans and danceable disco by disco fans.

Donna's response to this new musical development was quite remarkable. During the summer of 1979 she released a new album — *Bad Girls* — which established her as the first disco performer to cross over to rock. Two singles off the album — "Hot Stuff" and "Bad Girls" — clearly demonstrate Donna's abilities as a rock singer. A strong dance beat is still apparent on these cuts, but there are also several important new wrinkles.

Donna sings these songs with a tough street-wise attitude which demonstrates her skills as a blues-based rock singer. Even Moroder and Bellotte's production is much closer to hard-hitting R&B than to Eurodisco. If a record is defined by its substance rather than the public image of the artist, *Bad Girls* is closer to rock than to disco. Even the most hard core disco haters have been forced to acknowledge Donna's talent. This doesn't mean, however, that she is going to continue making records this way.

Now that Donna has clearly established her talent and versatility, she sees no reason to classify herself in any particular style. "Every song I do is not R&B or disco," she recently told *People* magazine. "We need to go back to categorizing songs instead of singers." There is much truth in these words. But Donna is well aware that all performers are classified. It is good to be versatile, but at some point it helps an artist to decide which direction she wishes to take.

In recent interviews, Donna has made it clear that she wants to break out of her disco sex-goddess image. The widespread acceptance of *Bad Girls* by rock fans should be a big help. But if she means to cultivate this audience, she must continue to make good records in this vein. She might also find it necessary eventually to split with her Eurodisco producers and find people to work with who can help her perfect a hard-hitting rock style.

But Donna isn't really worried about her musical direction. She is more concerned that the public accepts her as a real flesh-and-blood human being, not just a sex symbol. "Really I'm a very regular, normal person," she told *Penthouse*. "I want to relate to my audience . . . to let them know that I love them or I wouldn't be doing what I'm doing. At the same time, I want their love, respect and understanding."

DONNA SUMMER COLLECTORS' GUIDE
— Smash Hit

ALBUMS

Year	Album	Label	Hit
1975	Love to Love You Baby	Casablanca	*
1976	A Trilogy of Love	Casablanca	*
1976	Four Seasons of Love	Casablanca	*
1977	I Remember Yesterday	Casablanca	*
1977	Once upon a Time	Casablanca	*
1978	Live and More	Casablanca	*
1979	Bad Girls	Casablanca	*
1979	On the Radio — Greatest Hits Volume I and II	Casablanca	*

SINGLES

Year	Single	Label	Hit
1975	*Love to Love You Baby*	Casablanca	*
1976	*Spring Affair*	Casablanca	
1977	*Winter Melody*	Casablanca	
1977	*I Feel Love*	Casablanca	*
1977	*I Love You*	Casablanca	*
1978	*Rumor Has It*	Casablanca	
1978	*Last Dance*	Casablanca	*
1978	*MacArthur Park*	Casablanca	*
1978	*Heaven Knows*	Casablanca	*
1979	*Hot Stuff*	Casablanca	*
1979	*Bad Girls*	Casablanca	*
1979	*Dim All the Lights*	Casablanca	*
1979	*Enough Is Enough (No More Tears) (w/Barbra Streisand)*	Casablanca	*
1980	*On the Radio*	Casablanca	*

Singer-Songwriters

10. STEVIE WONDER

"My head hasn't swelled because I had success early. . . . Some of it has actually turned me off. I mean, there is a lot of bull that goes down in this business. People blowing money on cocaine when they could be giving it to those who need it. We artists owe more than our music to, like, black people. We should give them some time, and maybe some money too." (New York Post)

THE TERM "genius," has been too freely applied in the world of popular music over the past few years. Most often, the word is used by some record company publicist who is trying to "hype" a current artist. Many performers in the rock field have contributed great and lasting music, but this is not enough to qualify them for the lofty title of genius. In order to qualify, an artist must produce work with a quality and vision which goes beyond the abilities of other great people in the field. Stevie Wonder has clearly established himself as that kind of artist. He is probably the most influential black performer of his generation and an acknowledged musical genius.

Steveland Judkins Morris was born blind and poor on May 13, 1950, in Saginaw, Michigan. He was the third of six children fathered by different men. Even as a very young boy, Stevie never felt as though he were handicapped. He

Stevie Wonder at the keyboards
Record World—Motown Records

was such an active, happy child he hardly realized that he was missing something. One day when he was four, he got "whumped (by his mother) with the ironing chord for stepping in dog doo out in the back yard." At that point, it was explained to him that he had to take extra care when he was running around. Still, Stevie took part in most of the games that the other kids in his neighborhood were playing.

All through his early years, Stevie listened to many types

of music. There was the gospel music of the local Baptist church, which was what his family encouraged him to listen to. But Stevie was also attracted to the rhythm and blues sounds he was hearing on the black radio stations. This kind of music was having a golden era, and the youngster was exposed to the sounds of great performers such as Bobby "Blue" Bland, Ray Charles, Johnny Ace, Clyde McPhatter, B.B. King, and Jackie Wilson. He was rarely far from a radio during those years. Aside from his natural musical talent, Stevie's blindness caused him to develop an uncanny sense of hearing. He remembers people coming to his house and bouncing coins on the table, asking him to say whether it was a quarter, nickel or dime.

As he grew up, Stevie's musical world increased. He started at age three by making sounds with spoons. When Stevie was seven, the family moved to a housing project in Detroit. A friend of the family gave him his first musical instrument — a small harmonica. A neighbor had a piano and a set of toy drums which she let Stevie play. Within a year, he was well on his way to mastering all three instruments.

Stevie was also a great natural singer and a junior deacon at the local Baptist church. The older members of the church considered rock 'n' roll to be sinful music. But Stevie could not be held back. He would spend hours singing and playing with some friends on local porches, where crowds would often gather to hear the music. One day, an older member of the parish spotted Stevie playing in one of these jams, and after that he was no longer a Church deacon.

No matter, Stevie's young life was about to take its most important turn. One of his friends happened to mention the boy's many talents to Ronnie White, a member of a well-known singing group, the Miracles. An audition was set up with Motown Records, which at that time was called Hitsville, U.S.A. Berry Gordy, the company's owner, had a keen eye for talent. Although Stevie was only nine, he was immediately signed to a record contract. Gordy wanted his new artist to have a flashier name, and so Steveland Judkins Morris became Little Stevie Wonder.

For the next few years, Stevie spent as much time as he could hanging around the Motown studios. He occasionally got to play piano on gospel records. But mostly, he just listened and experimented with different instruments. His first song, "Lonely Boy," was written at ten, but his first hit record was not to come for another two years.

In 1963, Motown released an album of a live performance at Detroit's Regal Theatre — *Little Stevie Wonder the 12-Year-Old Genius*. This album contained the hit single, "Fingertips," which brought Stevie to national attention. Both the single and the album went all the way to the top of the charts that summer. Stevie's singing and harmonica playing had such intense energy, it sounded as though he were at the edge of his breath. Somehow, it was apparent that this was no one-shot artist. Stevie had a voice which belonged on the radio. He projected a joy which seemed to include and attract everybody.

Stevie's energy came off best in live performances. He became so involved in performing that he sometimes had to be physically removed from the stage. But there were also some problems during those years. The Detroit School Board wanted him to give up the music business and concentrate on his education. His popularity was now so great that his appearance on school grounds attracted fans and reporters and caused disruptions. Eventually, he was enrolled in the Michigan School for the Blind, and a schedule was arranged which allowed him to pursue his musical career.

For the next seven years, Stevie kept turning out hits. Many of these were in a similar snappy rhythm and blues vein like "Fingertips." Songs like "Uptight," and "I Was

Made to Love Her," were typical Motown dance hits. But he also made records which were not in the Motown mold. He was one of the first black artists to record songs by contemporary rock artists — like Bob Dylan's "Blowing in the Wind," and the Beatles' "We Can Work It Out." He also wrote his own material in a softer vein, such as "My Cherie Amour." All in all, Stevie's singles displayed more variety than those of any other Motown artist during the sixties. But it would be going too far to say that Stevie had true creative freedom in those years.

Motown Records was one of the first black-owned corporations to become a major power in American business. Berry Gordy, the company's founder and president, had an unmatched ability for finding talent and creating hits. A number of his greatest artists were discovered while they were young, and hungry for a chance to become stars. The contracts which they signed created a parent-child relationship between the record company and the artists. What this meant for Stevie was no control over his music or his money.

During his first ten years at Motown, Stevie earned one million dollars which was put in trust. This may seem like a huge sum, until you consider that he sold over thirty million dollars' worth of records during that time. Until he was twenty-one, Stevie received a small weekly allowance from Motown (reportedly $2.50 a week when he was thirteen). Many of the songs which he claims to have written were co-credited to other Motown writers. Also, he had little to say in the production of his records until the *Signed Sealed and Delivered* album in 1970. Before that, he pretty much did what Motown told him to do. He later told one reporter: "They would have the rhythm all worked out, and I would just come to the sessions and play the piano."

By the time he was twenty-one, Stevie had his fill of being

just another member of the "Motown family." He told one Motown executive: "I'm twenty-one now. I'm not going to do what you say any more. Void my contract." He then proceeded to invest several hundred thousand dollars in studio time in order to produce an album independently.

For the first time, Stevie had total control of his music and finances. He left Detroit and moved into a New York City hotel. He soon discovered the Moog and Arp synthesizers, which were to become the basis for his new sound. These synthesizers are actually keyboard computers which can duplicate the sounds of other instruments. By mastering these musical computers Stevie was able to make records almost completely by himself. On *Music of My Mind*, for example, he played all of the instruments with the exception of one guitar and one trombone solo. This gave his music a personal quality which has rarely if ever been matched in popular music.

Music of My Mind, more than any previous album, *is* Stevie Wonder. It is not just that he plays all the instruments and is the co-writer (together with ex-wife Syreta Wright) of all the songs that makes this record so personal. In between the notes and the lyrics, you can hear Stevie joking, laughing, and making an endless stream of sounds. Musically, the record owes as much to the Beatles' and jazz influences as it does to rhythm and blues. Stevie had taken his time and made an album that he felt pleased with. He was now ready to go back to Motown and talk business.

Although there have been many great artists at Motown, Stevie Wonder presented a special case. The range of his talent is so great that no record company could afford to let him slip away. Also, many of the proven Motown performers had either left the label or were no longer turning out hits. Stevie was in a position to get anything he wanted, and what he wanted was a lot of money and total creative freedom. The contract that Stevie and his lawyer Johannan

Vigoda worked out set a new standard in the entire business. Never had an artist been given such total creative control in addition to millions of dollars. Stevie probably could have gotten even more money from another company, but he decided to stay with Motown because — as he told a reporter from *Crawdaddy* — "It is a black company and I felt that we as a people needed something and had something that we could be proud of, and that it was representing a kind of music, a kind of contribution, that we had to give to America and to the world. It was a concept that I wanted to stay with and reinforce. It doesn't have anything to do with prejudice. It just deals with pride."

Stevie's next album, *Talking Book*, placed him back on the top of the charts for the first time in ten years. Not since "Fingertips," did Stevie have a number one single or album. But *Talking Book* topped the charts in 1973, and two singles off the album — "Superstition," and "You Are the Sunshine of My Life," — also made it to number one. In some respects, this album seemed to hark back to some of Stevie's earlier work. But now, Stevie's lyrics had become more complex, and he retained the synthesized sound of the Moog and Arp.

Talking Book proved one of the most influential albums of the early seventies. Stevie's popularity was now crossing all boundaries of age, race, and musical taste. He was winning Grammy Awards on one hand, and famous jazz musicians were copying his musical style on the other. One of these, guitarist George Benson, revived his career by singing like Stevie on songs such as "Masquerade." But in spite of his popularity, Stevie was still an opening act for The Rolling Stones on their American tour in 1972. There were some problems on the tour, but in the long run Stevie won over thousands of Rolling Stones fans. Everywhere he played his record sales soared.

Around the time that Stevie's next album — *Innervi-*

sions — was released, a car accident almost took his life. Stevie and his friend John Harris were driving down a North Carolina road when a truck loaded with logs collided with the car. One of the logs went right through the windshield and hit Stevie in the forehead. He was unconscious and bleeding profusely when they pulled him out of the wreck. For the next ten days, he lay in a coma in a hospital bed in Winston-Salem, North Carolina.

His road manager, Ira Tucker, was the first person to see Stevie show some sign that he would recover. Tucker told a reporter from *Esquire* magazine: "I remember when I got to the hospital in Winston-Salem . . . man I couldn't even recognize him. His head was swollen up about five times its normal size, and nobody could get through to him. I knew that he likes to listen to music really loud and I thought maybe if I shouted in his ear it might reach him. . . . The first time I didn't get any response, but the next day I went back and I got right down in his ear and sang 'Higher Ground.' His hand was resting on my arm and after awhile his fingers started going in time with the song. I said yeah! Yeeeeaaah! This dude is going to make it."

The road to recovery was long and hard, but Stevie did eventually make it. Aside from losing his sense of smell, he made a complete recovery and was performing within a few months. The accident seems to have made Stevie an even more spiritual person than he had been. One of the songs on the *Innervisions* album called "Higher Ground," spoke of receiving a second chance at life. Although the song was written before the accident, Stevie believes that he must have sensed that something was going to happen which would heighten his awareness. He told *Crawdaddy* magazine: "This is like my second chance for life, to do something or to do more, and to value the fact that I am alive."

Although *Innervisions* was released after the accident, it

was almost completely finished before that near-fatal day. At the time of its release, Motown Records invited a number of people for a prehearing of the album. This writer was one of those who went. Our host was the well known Motown singer-songwriter and executive, Smokey Robinson. He spoke about the album and then proceeded to pass out eye masks. He asked that we put the masks on so that we could experience the music without sight the way Stevie does. This did not work out so well, but it did bring up the question of how Stevie's blindness relates to his musical genius.

Stevie has called his blindness a "gift." In a sense, it is not difficult to understand what he means. Because he was always unable to see the outside world, he tended to look deeper inside himself than most people. In addition, he was able to develop his musical talent because he always needed to depend on hearing more than sighted people.

Those who know Stevie Wonder often speak of his lack of bitterness and his passion for life. Unlike many rock stars, he is truly humble about his success. He feels an intense and spiritual joy in his music which he sincerely wants to share with other people. Even his saddest ballads are somehow full of hope and joy. This spiritual side of his work has increased since the accident and his second marriage — to the former Yolanda Simmons.

On his 1974 album, *Fulfillingness First Finale*, Stevie combined his consummate professionalism with a heightened sense of joy. The album spawned two hit singles: the uptempo dance hit, "Boogie-on Reggae Woman," and the political, "You Haven't Done Nothin'." Both songs reached number one, and Stevie hit the peak of his life and his career. In conjunction with the album, he did an extensive tour which ended with a benefit at Madison Square Garden. Not only did Stevie bring the house down that night, he donated $50,000 to seven New York charities.

For the next two years, not much was heard about Stevie Wonder. There were no new records, live performances, or interviews. Now and then, there would be a magazine story about a trip to Africa or the birth of a baby daughter to Yolanda and Stevie. There was also some talk about an ambitious new album that Stevie was working on, but no official confirmation about a definite release date.

Finally, in 1976, a new double album, along with a small record and a book of commentary was released as *Songs in the Key of Life*. With so many musical and personal experiences under his belt, Stevie needed this big package to express it all. There were some familiar lyrical themes and musical sounds on this record, but there was also a good deal of experimentation. Stevie used jazz musicians on some songs, gospel choirs, and Hare Krishna groups on others. Before the album was even available in stores, it sold enough in prerelease orders to place it in the top five. Within two weeks of its official release, it replaced Peter Frampton's live album at the top of the charts and remained there for many months.

In essence, *Songs in the Key of Life* is a summing up of the second phase of Stevie's remarkable career. He was clearly established as the most talented and influential artist of the seventies. But at the same time, he had reached a saturation point in his musical direction. He needed something new and different, but this wasn't to come for another three years.

Stevie has so much talent that he must concern himself with the most productive ways to channel it. If he was only interested in turning out hit songs, he could probably have a new record on the charts every few weeks. But people have come to expect more from Stevie Wonder. And he expects more from himself. Stevie is a musical innovator who is honestly concerned with making records that are more than just commercial hits. That's why he sometimes takes years to make his albums. "I give a lot of respect to my fans," he told *Record World*. "I feel that if I cannot give them my best, I'll give them nothing at all."

In order to give his best, Stevie is always looking for new challenges. His most recent album — *Journey Through the Secret Life of Plants* — may have been the most difficult project he ever attempted. The music was originally conceived as a soundtrack for a film. "At first I thought I couldn't do it," he recalled. "I thought I should challenge the question of how a blind person could do music for a film. I just said, 'I'm sure there is a way I can do it.'"

The method Stevie used was to have someone describe the film to him through one channel of his headphones

Stevie Wonder—making great music since he was twelve
Record World—Tamla Records

while someone else read the film's narration through the other. It took a tremendous amount of time and effort for him to get the music just the way he wanted it, although there is still no definite release date for the film. But even if the movie is never shown, Stevie believes in the message of the music.

Outside of being a soundtrack, *Secret Life* is about more than the physical, mental, and emotional relationship between man and plants. It really deals with how all living things are bound together by one consciousness. I took that a little further and dealt with the fact that all cultures really have a connection.

Stevie strengthened these connections by using a number of natural sounds and foreign languages to get his point across. As he has done on much of his recent work, he wrote, produced, arranged, and played all musical instruments on the album. Compared to *Talking Book* or *Songs in the Key of Life, Journey Through the Secret Life of Plants* is more abstract and less commercial. But Stevie isn't worried about such things:

I want for (the album) to be successful, in the sense that people's minds are opening up and want to hear something like this. But then I also feel that it may not be as successful as some of the other records. And if that's so, I'm not going to feel bad about it. People say, "Well, you've got at least four potential hits," and I feel good about that. But I hope they go further than that. And I think people will.

STEVIE WONDER COLLECTORS' GUIDE

— Smash Hit

ALBUMS

Year	Album	Label	Hit
1963	Little Stevie Wonder 12-year-Old Genius	Tamla	*
1966	Uptight	Tamla	
1967	Down to Earth	Tamla	
1967	I Was Made to Love Her	Tamla	
1967	Someday at Christmas	Tamla	
1968	Stevie Wonder's Greatest Hits	Tamla	
1969	For Once in My Life	Tamla	
1969	My Cherie Amour	Tamla	
1970	Stevie Wonder Live	Tamla	
1970	Signed, Sealed and Delivered	Tamla	
1971	Where I'm Coming From	Tamla	
1971	Stevie Wonder's Greatest Hits Volume II	Tamla	
1972	Music of My Mind	Tamla	
1972	Talking Book	Tamla	*
1973	Innervisions	Tamla	*
1974	Fulfillingness First Finale	Tamla	*
1976	Songs in the Key of Life	Tamla	*
1979	Journey Through the Secret Life of Plants	Tamla	*

SINGLES

Year	Single	Label	Hit
1963	Fingertips	Tamla	*
1963	I Call It Pretty Music (Part I and Part II)	Tamla	
1963	Workout Stevie Workout	Tamla	

Year	Single	Label	Hit
1964	*Castles in the Sand*	Tamla	
1964	*Hey Harmonica Man*	Tamla	
1964	*Sad Boy*	Tamla	
1965	*Kiss Me Baby*	Tamla	
1965	*High Heel Sneakers*	Tamla	
1965	*Uptight (Everything's Alright)*	Tamla	*
1966	*Nothing's too Good for My Baby*	Tamla	*
1966	*Blowin' in the Wind*	Tamla	*
1966	*I'm Wondering*	Tamla	
1966	*A Place in the Sun*	Tamla	*
1966	*Someday a Christmas*	Tamla	*
1967	*Travelin' Man*	Tamla	
1967	*I Was Made to Love Her*	Tamla	*
1967	*I'm Wondering*	Tamla	*
1968	*Shoo-Be-Doo-Be-Doo-Da-Day*	Tamla	*
1968	*You Met Your Match*	Tamla	
1968	*For Once in My Life*	Tamla	*
1969	*I Don't Know Why*	Tamla	
1969	*My Cherie Amour*	Tamla	*
1969	*Yester-Me, Yester-You, Yesterday*	Tamla	*
1970	*Never Had a Dream Come True*	Tamla	
1970	*Signed Sealed Delivered I'm Yours*	Tamla	*
1970	*Heaven Help Us All*	Tamla	*
1971	*We Can Work It Out*	Tamla	*
1971	*Never Dreamed You'd Leave in Summer*	Tamla	
1971	*If You Really Love Me*	Tamla	*
1972	*Superwoman (Where Were You When I Needed You)*	Tamla	
1972	*Keep on Running*	Tamla	
1972	*Superstition*	Tamla	*
1973	*You Are the Sunshine of My Life*	Tamla	*
1973	*Higher Ground*	Tamla	*
1973	*Living for the City*	Tamla	*

Year	Single	Label	Hit
1974	Don't Worry 'bout a Thing	Tamla	*
1974	You Haven't Done Nothing	Tamla	*
1974	You Met Your Match	Tamla	
1974	Boogie on Reggae Woman	Tamla	*
1977	Sir Duke	Tamla	
1977	Another Star	Tamla	
1977	As	Tamla	
1977	Looking Back	Tamla	
1979	Send One Your Love	Tamla	*

Singer-Songwriters

11. ELTON JOHN

"This is my greatest achievement as an artist. I hope it will break down the barriers." (Elton commenting after his groundbreaking performance in Leningrad — May 21, 1979).

ELTON JOHN was the first rock superstar to put it all together in the seventies. He hit the scene at exactly the right moment. The Beatles had recently broken up, and the record industry was looking for some new blood to take up the slack. This is not to say that Elton replaced the Beatles, but there were some similarities between them. Like Lennon and McCartney, Elton and lyricist Bernie Taupin were able to write songs in a broad range of styles. Although Elton wrote and performed many full-tilt rockers, he was first identified with melodic ballads like "Your Song" and "Border Song." These records featured Elton's appealing pop-rock voice, accompanied by his flowing piano style. As the first major rock artist to perform with a trio centered around the piano rather than the guitar, Elton spawned a whole new generation of singing keyboard players.

Before he made his legendary American debut at the

Elton John—a wild and crazy singing piano player in the great tradition of Little Richard and Jerry Lee Lewis
Record World—MCA Records

Troubadour Club in West Hollywood on August 25, 1970, he was virtually unknown. Most peole had heard "Your Song," and found it pleasant enough. But who could have predicted the response that Elton and his group would receive. Although the Troubadour had previously showcased such major artists as Joni Mitchell and Kris Kristofferson, Elton created a level of excitement which immediately labeled him as *the* new superstar.

It is sometimes difficult to analyze exactly what it is that makes certain performers special. True, Elton John had a soulful voice and a unique instrumental sound. His songs covered a wide range of emotions, while they consistently retained an appealing commercial quality. Elton also displayed a dazzling sense of showmanship during his week-long engagement at the Troubadour. He was a rather pudgy looking fellow with a shy and humble personality. But Elton punctuated his performances with wild clothes, outlandish glasses, and push-ups on top of the piano. Elton recalled that he first developed his outrageous stage routine while trying to keep warm during a sub-freezing performance in Halifax:

> I've always been into Jerry Lee Lewis and Little Richard and all. So I started jumping around, not even really knowing what I was doing, and the crowd went bananas. I've kept it all in ever since and built on it. The audience gets a big kick out of it and so do I. People expect a good time. So I say, "Let's all go have a laugh and enjoy ourselves."

This feeling of pure fun and enjoyment had been missing from a rock scene that had begun to take itself too seriously. But Elton's stage antics ignited the Troubadour crowd. The room was full of musicians, critics, and music business heavies, but nobody could resist this balding childlike figure dressed in a Donald Duck bib, yellow overalls, and aluminum sparkle boots.

Elton's record company (Uni) had done a tremendous job in plugging and hyping their new artist. Record companies often attempt to launch new performers through expensive advertising campaigns, only to find that the performer is unable to live up to the promotion. But in the case of Elton John, all expectations were surpassed. The California rock press was beside itself with praise.

Rolling Stone called Elton's debut — "one of the greatest opening nights in Los Angeles rock."

The *Los Angeles Free Press* declared — "Elton John is a marvelous and very resourceful songwriter-performer."

The *Los Angeles Herald-Examiner* simply stated — "He is a spectacular talent."

Robert Hillburn, writing in the *Los Angeles Times*, was particularly ecstatic. "Rejoice!" he exclaimed. "Rock music, which has been going through an uneventful period lately, has a new star. He's Elton John, whose United States debut was in every way magnificent. . . . He's going to be one of rock's biggest and most important stars."

But Elton was less impressed with himself than others seemed to be. He was truly disturbed that the Troubadour audience paid no attention to the other performers who shared the bill with him — the Dillards, and David Ackles. "To see the audience just chatting away while he (Ackles) was singing those lovely songs just tore me apart," Elton recalled. "People were there because the word had gotten around that I was the guy to see, and they didn't give a toss about a great person like him."

All performers know how fickle and rude live audiences can sometimes be. But Elton was a performer who people just warmed to and cared about. His intelligence and sensitivity coupled with a unique kind of flash and outrageousness have made him one of the most beloved rock performers of all time. His reputation for dressing outlandishly and going on expensive buying sprees is well deserved. But Elton has understood the pitfalls of stardom from the beginning:

> That first week at the Troubadour was a great education for me. There were so many people who suddenly wanted to know me. Instantly I went from being a nobody to MR. ELTON JOHN. I must have shaken a million hands. People were slapping me on the back, calling me the great white wonder and all that.
>
> I was pretty naive before I came to America, but that week made me grow up. In that week, I must have seen all the con men and hypsters, and found that I could see through it all for the first time in my life. . . . I pledged myself not to end up like them.

Could it ever have occurred to the young, shy, chubby Reg Dwight (Elton's real name) that he would grow up to become one of rock's legendary performers? From the time he was three, Elton had been knocking out popular songs on the piano. His parents enrolled him at the London Royal Academy, but young Reg wasn't really interested in classical music. He vividly recalls the first time he really got excited about music. It was the day his mother brought him two early rock 'n' roll hits — Bill Haley's "ABC Boogie," and Elvis Presley's "Heartbreak Hotel."

> I remember she brought home the records and said they were different from what we had been hearing. Well, I couldn't believe how great they were. From then on, rock 'n' roll took over. I used to play Jerry Lee Lewis and Little Richard things on the piano, just thump them out.

In recalling his attitude towards schoolwork or his tedious classical piano exercises, Elton confesses that he didn't really give it his best:

> I was very lazy. So far as school or learning the piano, I never achieved what I could have because I knew I wanted to do something else. I wanted to sing like Elvis.

Reg's father — an officer in the Royal Air Force — was outraged when he learned of his son's plans to become a rock 'n' roll musician. Since Reg had always feared his strict father, he was not particularly upset when his parents got divorced. Mrs. Dwight was far more sympathetic to her son's plans and was relieved that she would no longer have to argue about this matter with her husband. But several months later, she received a letter from Officer Dwight which read: "Reggie must give up this idea of becoming a pop musician. He's turning into a wild boy. . . . Why can't he get a job as a banker or an executive for British Airways?"

But Elton's destiny lay elsewhere. While the divorce proceedings were taking place, the family was having difficulty making ends meet. So young Reg took weekend work at local clubs in order to help out. He soon accumulated enough money to buy an electric piano. At fourteen, he joined one of the many teenage bands that were forming throughout Great Britain and the United States. The quartet played at local parties and pubs. One of the highlights of their act was Elton's Jerry Lee Lewis takeoff. Lacking a real leader and the money to buy decent amplifiers, the group went the route of most high school bands. They broke up.

Several years later, a few of the band members got together again with some other young musicians. They were now a sextette working under the name Bluesology. The group was able to find work in a number of London's better clubs. Around this time, Elton heard that the Mills Publishing Company was looking for a boy to run errands and make tea. He immediately dropped out of his last term of high school and accepted the job. Between his gigs with Bluesology and his position at Mills, Reg felt that he was finally making some real progress in his musical career. Then, Elton recalls, Bluesology got its really big break:

An agent saw the band and asked if we'd be interested in backing American stars on tour in Britain. We were taken on to back Major Lance, which is when I quit my job at Mills. After Major Lance, we backed other R&B performers like Patti Labelle, Doris Troy, and Billy Stewart.

Elton had always been a great fan of American rhythm and blues. So naturally, he was thrilled to be working with people he numbered among his musical heroes. He also began to get work as a backup singer on low-cost copy versions of hit records. Meanwhile, a few of the members of Bluesology had quit, and the band was reduced to a trio.

One night in early 1967, the group was working at a popular musician's hangout — the Cromwellian Club. There they met a six-foot-seven-inch tall blues singing guitarist named Long John Baldry. During his ten-year career, Baldry had built a reputation as a good musician and an outrageous performer. When he asked Reg if Bluesology would consider becoming his backup group, there was little hesitation. Reg owned all of Baldry's records, and considered himself a fan. Playing with a bluesman like Baldry was exactly the kind of thing Elton had in mind.

Under the leadership of Long John Baldry, Bluesology was expanded to a nine-piece group, including horns and a female singer. Elton was given little opportunity to sing, but he was happy with the kind of music the group was playing. Bluesology was attracting good-size crowds wherever they played, though the record companies scarcely took notice. Baldry decided that the only way to get a record contract was to stop playing the blues, and try their luck with commercial pop music. Sure enough, the group's first record in this style — "Let the Heartaches Begin" — became an English hit. Reg was not at all happy with this turn of events. He hated this kind of music and the smart supper clubs that it attracted. It was now only a matter of time before he would leave the group.

Two major events took place before Reg up and left Bluesology. First, he decided to change his name from Reg Dwight to Elton John. His new name was derived from the first names of two Bluesology members — saxophone player Elton Dean, and bandleader Long John Baldry. Elton recalls his reasons for the change this way:

> I realized Reg Dwight was hopeless. It sounded like a library assisant. One of the guys in Bluesology was Elton Dean. I figured I could take part of his name but not all of it, or he'd kick up. Later I thought of changing it again, but nobody could come up with anything better.

The second major event that took place toward the end of Elton's tenure with Bluesology was an intense and near-disastrous relationship with a woman. One Christmas Eve at a club in Sheffield, Elton met a six-foot girl named Linda and entered into a volatile emotional relationship with her. Partially out of loneliness, Elton invited Linda to join him when the band moved on to its next engagement in South Shields. The two fell madly in love and got engaged.

Elton had so many problems with Linda during the next six months that his life must have seemed like a nightmare.

She hated everything about Reg — his friends, his clcthes, and especially his music. Linda wanted Reg to leave the music business and get a job in a bank. When she did not get her way, she would often become violent. Fortunately, Elton managed to back out of his marriage plans to Linda. One of his songs, "Someone Saved My Life Tonight," addresses itself to this experience:

Saved in time; thank God my music's still alive

Elton's relationship with Linda was clearly the low point of his life. He was so distraught that he even attempted suicide. "It was really a Woody Allen type suicide," Elton told *People* magazine. "I turned on the gas but left all of the windows open." To this day, Elton admits to "being wary of letting different women get to know me." The experience with Linda was so shattering that he never again formed another serious relationship with a woman.

Shortly after his near-disastrous engagement, Reg picked up a copy of the *New Musical Express* and spotted an ad that interested him greatly. Liberty Music was looking for singers, composers, and lyricists. He immediately called, and set up an audition. Elton vividly remembers that afternoon.

Liberty asked me to sing five songs, but all I knew was "He'll Have to Go," and "I Love You Because." I hadn't sung in years and I was awful. They turned me down, and I don't blame them.

As Elton was about to leave, one of the men auditioning him suggested that he look over some lyrics a young writer named Bernie Taupin had sent in. Perhaps he could find a way to set them to music. As far as Elton was concerned, any opportunity in the record business interested him. "I was impressed with Bernie's work," he recalls. "I was keen to team up with him, although the way I was feeling, I'd have been keen to team up with anyone."

Bernie Taupin was a seventeen-year-old high school dropout who had unsuccessfully tried to become a newspaper reporter. He had seen the ad in the *New Musical Express* and wrote a letter to Liberty with some of his poetry enclosed. On second thought, however, Bernie decided that his stuff wasn't good enough and tossed the letter in the wastebasket. Fortunately, Bernie's mother had more confidence in her son's writing abilities. She quickly retrieved the letter from the trash and mailed it.

Almost immediately, Elton was able to turn Bernie's words into songs. Soon Bernie was mailing his new writing partner more lyrics from his home in Lincolnshire. They wrote some two dozen songs without ever meeting each other. Although Elton regards these early efforts as "crude," they were published by the Hollies' music company.

Then, at the end of 1967, Elton was put in touch with the man who had first published the Beatles' music. Dick James had a small studio which he allowed promising artists to use. Caleb Quaye, a session guitarist, was working as an engineer at the studio. He liked Elton and Bernie's songs so much that he brought them to James's personal attention. Dick James was impressed enough to offer the pair a songwriting contract, and twenty-five dollars a week to make ends meet. But he did not envision Elton making it as an artist.

At that time, the thought of (Elton being an) artist was not in consideration because he was going into this "Micky Mouse" studio we had here that was merely a demo studio. But whenever we sat down to listen to Elton's material it was obvious that his talent was much beyond making a demo. We got the idea within a short while that no one was going to sing these songs better than he was singing them himself, because he was getting right inside them.

Apparently, it was Steve Brown — a promotion man for Dick James Music — who first encouraged Elton to write what he *felt* rather than gearing his songs for the top 40. A few weeks later, Elton and Bernie wrote "Lady Samantha." Brown produced the record, got it on the radio, and promoted it on his own. The record sold reasonably well for a first effort, and the London rock press gave it favorable reviews. Dick James decided to let Brown produce an entire album of Elton singing John-Taupin songs. The results were a sparsely arranged, energetic record — *Empty Sky*. Although the album was a critical success, Elton recalls that he still wasn't making much money.

> I wasn't doing gigs. I didn't have a band together. In fact . . . "Lady Samantha" was a turntable hit, not a financial success. And then, "It's Me You Need" came out, followed by "Empty Sky." They also got good reviews and didn't sell.

In the meantime, Dick James and his son Stephen were trying to find an American record company to release *Empty Sky*. The only record executive to express any interest in the album was Russ Regan of Uni Records, now called MCA. Back in London, Elton had teamed up with producer Gus Dudgeon to complete a second LP — *Elton John*. Stephen James remembers that when Regan heard this album: "He hit the ceiling, he went berserk, thought it was incredible, and wanted to make a deal."

It was Regan who arranged Elton's groundbreaking week at the Troubadour. At the time, Stephen James still wasn't sure if Elton was ready to handle a major debut.

He hadn't done a lot of work, but he had developed a make-shift group with (drummer) Nigel Olson and (bass guitarist) Dee Murray.

Russ said that a friend of his at the Troubadour had offered a support situation to Elton and his group, but that the money would be very low indeed, and wouldn't cover his expenses. Nevertheless, he'd offered him a week in Los Angeles and a week in San Francisco, and it was the best he could do. Russ thought it would be the perfect situation to show off Elton to the press, and get the publicity he required to release the record. Of course, no one at the time was expecting anything sensational.

But as we have seen, Elton's debut was more than sensational. Within a few weeks of his triumph at the Troubadour, the word was out: Elton John was *the new superstar*. Publicist Norm Winter remembers the kind of promotion Elton's first American tour received. "We treated him as if it was an Elvis Presley opening in Vegas, though nobody had ever heard of Elton John. People all over began to say: 'My God, what is an Elton John? A toilet?' "

By 1971, everyone knew who Elton John was. He had done a soundtrack for a film called *Friends*, and another album — *Tumbleweed Connection*. In addition, a live performance at a tiny studio of New York radio station WABC was recorded and released under the title, *11-17-70*. Along with the *Elton John* LP, he now had four albums on the charts at the same time. The last artists to have achieved this kind of commercial success were the Beatles.

Now that Elton was finally reaping fame and fortune, he found that some members of the rock press had turned against him. On early records like "Your Song," "Country Comfort," and "Levon," Elton came across like a laid-back folk-rock singer. People somehow expected him to be quiet

Elton John—one of rock's best, and most flamboyant, performers.
Record World—MCA Records

and introverted. In fact, he is that way a good deal of the time. But Elton decided he wanted a different image on-stage. He genuinely believed that rock 'n' roll performances should be dynamic, but he also had personal reasons for becoming an outrageous showman.

> I had a bad childhood. Really, it took a lot out of me. My mother was everything to me . . . but I used to pray that my father wouldn't come home weekends. I was fat . . . and I had a terrible inferiority complex. That's why I'm outrageous on-stage . . . and that's why I wear such ridiculous clothes. My clothes just make up for lost time. I didn't even start living until I was twenty-three so I suppose I'm just making up for it now. My life is just an extension of things I always wanted to do. Bright clothes and shiney things. I'm catching up for all the games I missed as a child; I'm releasing myself.

This is a most unusual confession for a rock star, and an important key to why Elton is so loved by his fans. Cheering for this vulnerable hero is something like rooting for the underdog. There is something very human and touching about a flashy rock star who admits to being afraid of girls. One only needs to hear Elton speak to know that he is sincere about all of this. It isn't as though he is trying to exploit the image of the *poor little rich kid*. Somehow it comes across naturally. But not everyone was turned on by Elton's on-stage antics. Here is a typical negative review of an Elton John performance which sums up the complaints of most of his detractors.

> John substitutes imitation for originality in both his music and his stage antics. . . . At one point in the concert, the musician in Elton John gave way to the showman. When John threw his long coattails into the audience and took off his silver boots, and climbed his piano, it was like a cheerleader at

his first rally.... If John takes his performance seriously, that's one thing. But if he asks others to accept this neatly-packaged, glossed-over and well promoted garbage ... then music has become nothing more than slick packaging and an energetic advertising campaign.

Serious rock fans as well as critics have often had a problem defining Elton's music. At times, he has displayed the characteristics of the most highly regarded rock artists. A number of his writing efforts with Taupin, such as "Your Song," "Rocket Man," and "Bennie and the Jets," are rock classics. But some of his records were little more than gimmicky top-40 products. "Crocodile Rock" — Elton's first number-one hit — stands out as the most obvious. But Elton has always been a great lover of all kinds of rock. It is well known that he buys every single on the top 100, and is often referred to as the "consummate rock fan."

Elton John is one of those artists that people tend to overreact to. While some condemn him as a commercial sellout, others hail him as a great genius. The truth lies somewhere in between. Elton is a *good* singer and a *good* songwriter. He is a highly creative performer and recording artist with a number of very good records to his credit. Although most of his albums up until 1976 were best-sellers, he is usually identified with his singles. Some of the best include: "Daniel," from *Don't Shoot Me I'm Only the Piano Player*; "Bennie and the Jets," from *Goodbye Yellow Brick Road*, and "The Bitch is Back," from *Caribou*.

In 1975, Elton replaced Dee Murray and Nigel Olson with Kenny Passareli on bass and Roger Pope on drums. He retained guitarist Davey Johnstone and added old friend Caleb Quaye on rhythm guitar, Ray Cooper on percussion, and James Newton Howard on keyboards. The group was soon in the studio recording *Rock of the Westies*, Elton's tightest and toughest rock album to date.

Between 1971–1976, Elton was the most successful artist in rock. His tours broke records set by Elvis, and the Rolling Stones. He consistently sold out indoor arenas such as New York's Madison Square Garden, and outdoor ballparks such as Los Angeles's Dodger Stadium, with guaranteed regularity.

When people in the music business talk about Elton John, they mention his professionalism and his wide appeal. One promoter remarked that Elton's audiences include, "hippies, film stars, lords and ladies, teenagers, and people in their forties." Guitarist Caleb Quaye feels that Elton's greatest strength lies in the freshness of his music, and he adds: "There's something for all kinds of people to hear — it's not just rock. There's music for every age to relate to plus there are costumes for the kids and what have you. . . . But the music has always been good, which I think has lent a lot of substance and strength to the whole thing."

But in spite of the quality of his music, Elton has received much more publicity for his flashy performances and his unusual lifestyle. In 1974, Elton signed a colossal eight-million-dollar contract with MCA. He now had so much money that he almost had to try to invent new ways of spending it. Aside from acquiring a majority interest in an English soccer team — the Watford Hornets — Elton is well known for his interest in rare works of art and classic automobiles. He is also famous for owning some 200 pairs of glasses valued at over forty thousand dollars. These include several pairs that are mink lined, and others that spell out the name "Elton" in diamonds. In the tradition of Elvis Presley, Elton has been reported to have spent thousands of dollars on gifts for friends and associates.

After he became established as an artist, he displayed an interest in becoming a businessman. In 1974, he launched his own company, Rocket Records, in order to work with other artists. He produced hits with English singer Kiki Dee and helped American singer-songwriter Neil Sedaka stage a successful comeback. In his typically generous fashion, Elton gave all the artists on his label an unusually high royalty rate. But as one executive for Rocket Records points out, Elton is a knowledgeable and skillful businessman:

> Elton is very aware of all facets of the music business. For example, he understands everything about the American radio situation. He takes an active part in the way Rocket goes. In the case of Kiki Dee and Neil Sedaka . . . he went and did interviews, promoting them more than himself. He knew that he didn't have to sell himself, so he was out there promoting other Rocket artists.

In 1975, Elton expanded his horizons even further. He made his movie debut — appearing as the Pinball Wizard in the film version of The Who's rock opera, Tommy. His records were still on top of the charts, and he was recognized as the biggest live attraction in rock. Around this time though, Elton began to express some doubts about his position as a superstar. He made a number of statements indicating that he would soon change his lifestyle:

> I'm at the top of the heap. . . . But I won't be singing "Crocodile Rock" in six year's time. I don't want to become a pathetic rock-'n'-roller and take a slow climb down like a lot of people do. When I'm forty, I don't want to be charging around the countryside doing concerts. My real ambition in life is to retire and become chairman of my favorite soccer team — the Watford Hornets.

During the summer of 1976, Elton had made up his mind to give up touring indefinitely, perhaps forever. In a now famous interview with Rolling Stone, he revealed that he was bisexual and expressed an intense need to find somebody

of either sex to, "share all this with." Elton proceeded to re-
tire from the music business, referring to his rock star's existence as a "Disney film."

For the next two years, Elton became one of rock's most
invisible superstars. He had stopped performing completely, and his records soon disappeared from the charts.
But in the spring of 1979, he staged a unique comeback. Accompanied only by percussionist Ray Cooper, Elton became
the first major rock artist to perform in the USSR. The Rus-
sian kids turned out by the thousands to give Elton a wildly
ecstatic response. He then announced that he would tour
America the following fall.

In his first series of American concerts since 1976, Elton
once again performed solo, except for Cooper's occasional
percussion. Rock performers almost never perform without
a full band, but Elton proved equal to the challenge. In an
attempt to achieve a more intimate contact with his audiences, Elton deserted the large arenas and stadiums for
smaller, cozier halls. As he played and sang his hits with
conviction and fire, he left little doubt that his skills as a
performer are still intact. But Elton's most recent albums
have raised some questions about his ability to turn out new
material that comes up to the best of his earlier work.

Elton's two last records in the 1970's — *The Thom Bell Sessions* and *Victim of Love* were his first efforts without Bernie
Taupin. Although critics often panned Taupin's songwriting as "gimmicky and pretentious," his lyrics provided an
essential building block for the Elton John sound. Without
the proper lyrics, Elton seemed to be groping for a new direction. But in the spring of 1980, he released a new album,
21 at 33. This record was his best and most successful effort
since *Rock of the Westies.* Featured are four new John-Taupin
compositions, as well as collaborations with Tom Robinson,
Judie Tzuke, and Gary Osborne. It looks as if Elton is making a serious comeback. But just how far can he go in the
eighties?

"He's still a great entertainer," Lester Bangs wrote in the *Village Voice.* "If he finds himself — or maybe even just the right lyricist — again, there's no reason why his second decade shouldn't be as bountiful as his first."

Let's hope so. The radio could use more of Elton John at his best. And so could the millions of fans who consider him their favorite rock performer.

ELTON JOHN COLLECTORS' GUIDE
* — *Smash Hit*

ALBUMS

Year	Album	Label	Hit
1970	Elton John	Uni	*
1971	Tumbleweed Connection	Uni	*
1971	Friends (Soundtrack)	Paramount	
1971	11-17-70	Uni	*
1971	Madman across the Water	Uni	*
1972	Honky Chateau	Uni	*
1973	Don't Shoot Me I'm Only the Piano Player	MCA	*
1973	Goodbye Yellow Brick Road	MCA	*
1974	Caribou	MCA	*
1974	Elton John's Greatest Hits	MCA	*
1975	Empty Sky	MCA	*
1975	Captain Fantastic and the Brown Dirt Cowboy	MCA	*
1975	Rock of the Westies	MCA	*
1976	Here and There	MCA	*
1976	Blue Moves	Rocket	*
1977	Elton John Greatest Hits Volume II	MCA	*

Year	Album	Label	Hit
1978	Elton — It's a Little Bit Funny	MCA	*
1978	A Single Man	MCA	
1979	The Thom Bell Sessions (45 extended play)	MCA	
1979	Victim of Love	MCA	
1980	21 at 33	MCA	*

SINGLES

Year	Single	Label	Hit
1968	I've Been Loving You	Uni	
1969	Rock 'n' Roll Madonna	Uni	
1969	Lady Samantha	Uni	
1970	Border Song	Uni	
1970	Your Song	Uni	*
1971	Friends	Uni	
1971	Levon	Uni	
1971	Tiny Dancer	Uni	
1972	Rocket Man	Uni	*
1972	Honky Cat	Uni	*
1972	Crocodile Rock	MCA	*
1973	Daniel	MCA	*
1973	Saturday Night's Alright for Fighting	MCA	*
1973	Goodbye Yellow Brick Road	MCA	*
1973	Step into Christmas	MCA	
1974	Bennie and the Jets	MCA	*
1974	Don't Let the Sun Go Down on Me	MCA	*
1974	The Bitch Is Back	MCA	*
1974	Lucy in the Sky with Diamonds	MCA	*
1975	Philadelphia Freedom	MCA	*
1975	Someone Saved My Life Tonight	MCA	*
1975	Island Girl	MCA	*

Year	Single	Label	Hit
1975	Grow Some Funk of Your Own	MCA	
1976	With Your Love	MCA	
1976	St. Charles	MCA	
1976	Don't Go Breaking My Heart (w/Kiki Dee)	MCA/Rocket	*
1976	I Feel Like a Bullet	MCA	
1976	Sorry Seems to be the Hardest Word	MCA/Rocket	*
1977	Bite Your Lip	MCA	
1978	Ego	MCA	
1978	Part Time Love	MCA	
1979	Victim of Love	MCA	
1979	Johnny B-Goode	MCA	
1980	Little Jeannie	MCA	*

Bibliography

BELZ, CARL. *The Story of Rock.* New York: Oxford University Press, 1969.

BUSNAR, GENE. *It's Rock 'n' Roll.* New York: Julian Messner, 1979.

DALTON, DAVID. *Janis.* New York: Popular Library Edition, 1971.

DAVIES, HUNTER. *The Beatles* (Revised edition of the authorized biography). New York: McGraw Hill Book Company, 1968.

DRAGONWAGON, C. *Stevie Wonder.* New York: Flash Books, 1977.

DUNLEAVY, STEVE, with Red West, Sonny West, and Dave Hebler. *Elvis—What Happened?* New York: Ballantine Books, 1977.

FRIEDMAN, MYRA. *Buried Alive: The Biography of Janis Joplin.* New York: Bantam Books, 1974.

GILLET, CHARLIE. *The Sound of the City.* New York: Outerbidge and Dienstfrey, 1970.

GOLDSTEIN, RICHARD. *Goldstein's Greatest Hits.* Englewood Cliffs, New Jersey: Prentice Hall, Inc., 1970.

JASPER, TONY. *The Rolling Stones.* London: Octopus Books, 1976.

LYNDON, MICHAEL. *Rock Folk. New York: Dial Press, 1971.*

MARCUS, GREIL. *Mystery Train*. New York: Dutton, 1976

NEWMAN, GERALD, with Joe Bivong. *Elton John*. New York: Signet Book/New American Library, 1976.

NITE, NORM. N. *Rock On Volume I*. New York: Thomas Y. Crowell, 1974.

————. *Rock on Volume II*. New York: Thomas Y. Crowell, 1978.

PALMER, TONY. *All You Need Is Love*. New York: Grossman Publishers Division of Viking Press, 1976.

The Rolling Stone Illustrated History of Rock and Roll. Edited by Jim Miller. New York: Random House Books. Rolling Stone Press, 1976.

The Rolling Stone Interviews Volume I. Edited by the Editors of *Rolling Stone*. New York: Warner Paperback Library, 1971.

The Rolling Stone Interviews Volume II. Edited by Ben Fong Torres. New York: Warner Paperback Library, 1973.

The Rolling Stone Rock 'n' Roll Reader. Edited by Ben Fong Torres. New York: Bantam Books, 1974.

ROXON, LILLIAN. *Lillian Roxon's Rock Encyclopedia*. New York: Universal Library/Grosset and Dunlop, 1971.

SHAW, ARNOLD. *The World of Soul*. New Jersey: Cowles Book Company, 1970.

STAMBLER, ERWIN. *The Encyclopedia of Pop, Rock and Soul*. New York: St. Martins Press, 1974.

STEVENS, KIM. *The Bee Gees*. New York: Quick Fox, 1977.

SWENSON, JOHN. *The Beatles Yesterday and Today*. New York: Zebra Books/Kensington Publishing Corporation, 1978.

WHITBURN, JOEL. *Record Research*, based on *Billboard* magazine, 1949–1971.

Index

About the Author

DURING THE 60's and 70's, Gene Busnar was involved in almost every phase of the music business. He was a member of a number of popular bands in New York and Philadelphia which opened for name artists like Cream, Van Morrison, Chicago, and B.B. King. He was signed as a songwriter by Edwin H. Morris Inc. and Famous Music Inc., and produced, arranged, and played on many recording sessions. In 1974, Gene turned his attentions to writing. His magazine credits include *Bananas, Alternate Currents, Today's Jogger,* and *CMJ*. He is currently living in New York City where he works as a writer. He has done a number of radio interviews, and frequently reviews and writes about contemporary music. His first book, *It's Rock 'n' Roll,* is regarded as one of the most comprehensive discussions of the development of early rock styles. Gene is presently working on a third book, *The Rhythm and Blues Story.*